Talking Donkeys
and
Wheels of Fire

—

Bible Stories That Are Truly Bizarre!

J. STEPHEN LANG

WARNER
Faith

A Division of AOL Time Warner Book Group

Unless otherwise indicated, Scripture quotations are from the HOLY BIBLE: NEW INTERNATIONAL VERSION®. Copyright © 1973, 1978, 1984 by International Bible Society. Used by permission of Zondervan Publishing House. All rights reserved.
Scriptures noted RSV are taken from the REVISED STANDARD VERSION of the Bible. Copyright © 1946, 1952, 1971, 1973 by the Division of Christian Education of the National Council of the Churches of Christ in the U.S.A. Used by permission.
Scriptures noted KJV are taken from THE KING JAMES VERSION of the Bible.
Scriptures noted NRSV are taken from the NEW REVISED STANDARD VERSION of the Bible. Copyright © 1989 by the Division of Christian Education of the National Council of the Churches of Christ in the U.S.A. All rights reserved.
Scriptures noted ESV are taken from The Holy Bible, English Standard Version, copyright © 2001 by Crossway Bibles, a division of Good News Publishers. Used by permission. All rights reserved.
Scriptures noted JEB are taken from THE JERUSALEM BIBLE. Copyright © 1966 by Darton, Longman & Todd Ltd. and Doubleday & Company, Inc. Used by permission.
Scriptures noted AP are author's paraphrase.

Warner Books, Inc., 1271 Avenue of the Americas, New York, NY 10020
Visit our Web site at www.twbookmark.com

W WARNER *Faith*™   A Division of AOL Time Warner Book Group

Printed in the United States of America

First Warner Books printing: September 2003

10   9   8   7   6   5   4   3   2   1

Library of Congress Cataloging-in-Publication Data

Lang, J. Stephen
   Talking donkeys and wheels of fire : Bible stories that are truly bizarre! / J. Stephen Lang.
      p. cm.
   ISBN 0-446-69067-8
   1. Bible stories, English. I. Title.

BS550.3.L36 2003
220.9'505—dc21   2003043286

Contents

Introduction vii

Beastly King 1

Israelite Meets Cellulite 4

Honey-Baked Lion, or Lion-Baked Honey 7

Hot Wheels 9

Curse That Donkey 11

The Great Artemis Pep Rally 14

Brimstone Central 17

Wormy Herod 19

The Ark, Pre-Hollywood 22

The Child-Eating Hell God 25

Raising Cain a Wife 28

Moses' Snakebite Cure 30

The One and Only Original Scapegoat 33

Sons of God, Human Beauties—and Fallen Giants 36

Moses the Mountain Goat 38

The Maltese Viper 41

Dancing for Fun and Prophet 44

Sibling Deviltry 46

The Ultimate Dysfunctional Family 49

Saul the Heretic 52

Mountain of Metamorphosis 55

The Original Camel Jockeys 58

Peter's Rooftop Buffet 60

The Big Wedding Night Switcheroo 62

The Seven-Day Wonder of Israel 64

Red or Reed, Awesome Either Way 67
Revisiting the Tongues-of-Fire Story 71
Reptilian Chitchat 74
Striking Down the Number One Son 76
Herod the Great (Killer) 80
Saul, Paul, Paulus, Etc. 82
Pinned to the Mat by God 85
The Small Poultry and "What Is It?" Diet 87
Unicorns? Really? 91
The Prostitute's Son, and His Poor Daughter 94
A Splitting (Literally) Headache 97
Window to Heaven 99
Jonah, the Runaway Prophet 102
The Samson Angel, Up in Smoke 106
The Daniel Diet 108
The Syrian Skin Man 112
Raising the Roof (Literally) 115
Call Him "Hash" for Short 117
Old Sol, Stopped Dead in Its Tracks 120
Gray-Bearded Cheerleader 123
As Old as . . . You Know Who 126
Fleecing the Lord 128
Hot Pillar, Smoky Pillar 131
Leviathan, and Other Fearsome Things 135
Heavenly Porter, with Attitude 138
It's Cool in the Furnace 139
Blood Flood 142
Lying and Dying 147
Goaded to War 150
Making a Fire in the Desert 152
The Knock-Kneed King of Persia 155
The Old Testament's Teetotaling Hippies 158
Righteous Noah—Well, Usually 160
Great Special Effects—Ancient Israel Style 162
Heads Are Gonna Roll 164
The Old Testament Trinity 166
Yep, That Old Lions' Den Story 168

Death by Eunuch   172
Not Exactly Cupid's Arrow   175
Tamar and the World's First ID Bracelet   178
The Unheard-of Sin of Gibeah   180
Rocking Out the Water   183
Jesus Cursing?   186
A Relative Matter   188
Gabriel the Tongue-Stopper   190
Why de Walls Come Tumblin' Down   193
Smooth Man Versus Bear Man   196
Assyrian Death in Massive Doses   199
A Truly Heavenly Spa   202
Isaiah's Temple Trip   204
Dropping Dead, After a Deadly Drop   206
The Lord Giveth, the Lord Taketh   208
Zeke and the Extraterrestrials   210
Israel's King, Naked (But Not Really)   213
Outfoxing the Philistines   215
The Valley of Dem Bones, Dem Bones, Dem Dry Bones   217
The Leprosy Lady   219
Peck Up Your Groceries   223
Organic (and Recycled) Food in Famine Time   225
The Ancient Version of Workplace Theft   227
Earthly Powers Versus the Rebels   230

Introduction

The Good Book, and Its Many Oddities

News of the Weird" is the name of a popular syndicated newspaper column. Apparently many readers (myself included) enjoy the various offbeat, off-the-wall news tidbits in this column, items that make the "normal" news seem pretty tame and pretty dull by comparison. Many of the column's tidbits fit into the "man bites dog" category—items that get the reader's attention and cause him to exclaim, "Well, ain't that peculiar!"

The Bible, also known as the Holy Bible, the Word of God, and sacred Scripture, has its share of "Ain't that peculiar!" items. Its many authors, spread out over many centuries, did not write to amuse readers, of course. The Bible authors wrote to inspire, to remind people that God ruled the world and that people ought to respond accordingly, living a life of faith. But its authors were also aware (as all authors are) that the weird, the bizarre, the offbeat can grab and hold the reader's attention.

The Gospels, for example, tell the story of a mysterious event known as the Transfiguration, in which the very human Jesus suddenly appeared "in glorious splendor" (Luke 9:31) and conversing with two long-dead saints from the distant past. No doubt the Gospel writers told this story for two reasons: it actually happened, and it was so odd and puzzling that it grabs the reader's interest in a dramatic way.

Another example: In the Old Testament's book of Judges, the story is told of an Israelite military leader, Ehud, who devised a clever scheme to murder the king of Moab. The story adds the odd detail that this king was so obese that Ehud's sword was literally lost inside all the fat. Why did the author include this detail? Probably because it was true, and also because it adds a lot of color to an already colorful story. If you ever read the Judges account of Ehud, you will never forget the detail about the fat king of Moab. (Call it the "Israelite Meets Cellulite" story.)

The Bible is full to the brim with such stories. Good preachers and Sunday school teachers know this, and they know it is easy to get kids interested in the Bible because all these oddities are wonderful "hooks" that naturally grab the kids' attention and hold it. Yet sometime in life, people somehow start believing the Bible is a boring book—which is certainly not the case. Adults, young and old, need to be reminded that the Bible is not only the inspired word of God, but also a very interesting book, written by human beings and for human beings, and full of very odd incidents and characters.

And that is what this book is all about: introducing (or reintroducing) you to some of the most peculiar incidents in the Bible. Some may be familiar, others may not. Taken individually or together, they should convince you that this book written in ancient times can still capture the attention of a twenty-first-century reader.

One of the aims of this book is to amuse you. The other is to inspire you. As bizarre as some of these incidents are, each of them has a spiritual or moral lesson. And it would be, frankly, unfair to the Bible and its original authors to present these many oddities to you without giving you some take-home value that you can apply to your own life.

So, welcome to the wide, wild, weird world of the Bible. I hope you enjoy reading about these odd episodes as much as I enjoyed writing about them.

Beastly King

Ruler of one of the world's great empires—eating grass like a cow

People who say the Bible is all legend are all wrong. Many of the people in it are well known to historians. Among these is one of the most renowned kings of ancient times, Nebuchadnezzar of Babylon. He was a force to be reckoned with, and the history books give us many details about his life and conquests. But only the Bible contains the story of the proud and mighty king going thoroughly insane. The one who was resplendent on the gilded throne of power became like a beast of the field.

We get our first glimpse of Nebuchadnezzar in 2 Kings 25. He did what powerful rulers did in those days: made war on other nations, conquered them, and made slaves of the people. His armies laid siege to Jerusalem, the capital of Israel. Zedekiah, king in Jerusalem, attempted to flee the city, but the Babylonians captured him. They slaughtered his sons right before his eyes, then blinded him and took him in chains to Babylon. Kings in those days did not mind being called "mean-spirited"—in fact, they loved to be feared. Their chief pleasure in life was flying the pennants of their pride.

The Babylonians burned the king's palace in Jerusalem and, even worse, the temple of God. They left only the poorest people in the area and carted the leading citizens off to Babylon. This was standard procedure: if you conquered an area, you were wise to get rid of the people who would likely try to revolt against you. They took those people to Babylon, too far away to hatch a conspiracy in Israel.

This happened in 586 B.C., a date worth remembering, for the Israelites never forgot the destruction of the famous temple that Solomon

1

had built. Even while living in exile in Babylon, they never stopped thinking about Jerusalem.

One of the Israelites deported to Babylon was Daniel, whose story appears in the book that bears his name. The Babylonians chose Daniel, who was young and bright, to serve in the king's court. Again, this was a prudent use of conquered people: choose the best ones to serve you, get some use out of them, and at the same time wean them away from their homeland and the religion they had embraced all their lives. Many young men in such circumstances would do the obvious thing: convert to the culture and religion of their conquerors. Daniel didn't. He stayed faithful to his God even while waiting on the idol-worshiping king of Babylon.

Daniel had an ability that dazzled people in the ancient world: he could interpret dreams. This puzzles us today, because we wonder: when someone claimed to interpret a dream, how did the person with the dream know that this was the *correct* interpretation? We don't know. The Bible doesn't tell us. Perhaps there was something in the interpreter's face or voice that seemed extremely convincing. We only know that when Daniel spoke, Nebuchadnezzar listened.

Chapter 4 of Daniel tells us that Nebuchadnezzar had a dream that baffled all his Babylonian court soothsayers. So he turned to Daniel, who learned that the king dreamed of an enormous tree, whose "top reached to heaven" (Dan. 4:11 RSV). In the dream, a heavenly being ordered the tree cut down, with its branches lopped off and its leaves and fruit stripped away.

Daniel understood the dream, but he knew the interpretation wouldn't please the king. The tree was, of course, Nebuchadnezzar himself. He was going to be "cut down"—not killed, but driven from his throne. Oddly, the Bible does not tell us how the king reacted to this news. It says only that in twelve months he was walking on his palace roof, boasting to himself of his power and wealth, when suddenly he was "driven from among men, and ate grass like an ox, and his body was wet with the dew of heaven till his hair grew long as eagles' feathers, and his nails were like birds' claws" (Dan. 4:33 RSV). He was, eventually, restored to his sanity and his throne—but only after he acknowledged that God ruled, and that God was able to humble the proud.

What happened to him during this "beastly" period? Obviously he was insane. Psychologists are aware of certain forms of schizophrenia in which a person believes himself to be an animal, and acts accordingly. We don't know what triggered this, mentally or physically. The Bible gives us the spiritual meaning: the proud king who conquered nations and held sway over an empire faced God's punishment, which made him less than human. He regained his power when he admitted that men are not gods, that only God is supreme.

Only the Bible mentions Nebuchadnezzar's madness. Does this mean it never really happened? Not at all. Certainly the Babylonian court chronicles would not have recorded such an embarrassing incident. The Babylonians would have kept the story hushed up, while the people of Israel would have passed it on, since it taught a wonderful moral: God can humble the proud—as happened to the proud Babylonian who sacked Jerusalem and burnt God's temple. Nebuchadnezzar was neither the first nor last arrogant soul to fall from a great height.

If you like browsing the Internet, find your favorite search engine and type in "William Blake Nebuchadnezzar." This will lead you to websites where you can view the famous picture of mad Nebuchadnezzar drawn by the English artist William Blake. If you've ever seen Blake's image of the long-haired, long-nailed, wild-eyed, naked king down on all fours, it will stick in your memory. Blake could have given it the caption: "This is what pride leads to."

Israelite Meets Cellulite

Left-handed sword meets a very fat king

If there is a book of the Bible with an *in*appropriate name, it has to be Judges. We think of judges as solemn-looking persons wearing black robes and presiding over courtrooms. These are certainly not the people who are at center stage in the book of Judges. Its main characters were military deliverers, heroic men who helped fight off Israel's many oppressive pagan neighbors. No judge in a black robe could do this. Israel needed men of action, men willing to pick up a sword and charge into battle. There was no king in those days, so Israel had to rely on charismatic leaders whom God would raise up at particular times to deliver them from foreign invaders and oppressors.

The Hebrew title of the book is *Shophetim*, which means something like "deliverers" or "leaders." When the book was translated into Latin, it was given the name *Judicum*, roughly meaning "the ones who bring justice." Alas, this passed into English as "judges." It would be much more appropriate to call it "Heroes" or "Deliverers," but after hundreds of years we are stuck with calling it Judges.

When you read in the book that "Tola judged Israel twenty-three years," be aware that Tola wasn't sitting in a courtroom wearing a robe, but rather, was out fighting Israel's enemies. Some newer translations are more on target when they say "led" instead of "judged."

Whatever you call the judges, they were an impressive group of men—and one woman as well. (More about her in a later chapter.) As you might expect, the book is extremely violent, with a smattering of illicit sex, too. These were violent times, and if Israel's leaders were men of the sword, this was necessary, for Israel's neighbor countries in the region of Canaanite were not exactly nonviolent themselves.

You don't have to read far in Judges before you realize certain formulas appear again and again. A section will begin: "The Israelites did evil in the eyes of the LORD" and then follows one of the pagan nations' oppression of Israel. Then God raises up a deliverer, someone he empowered by his Spirit to lead the Israelite men to war. Peace comes, but then the formula repeats itself once more: "The Israelites did evil in the eyes of the LORD."

Let's pause for a moment and ask the obvious question: what evil were they doing? Simply put, they were worshiping the gods of the pagans, not the true God of Israel. In our tolerant modern age, that sounds like a minor thing. Wasn't one god as good as another? No one in the ancient world looked at it that way, and certainly the more moral among the Israelites did not. There was only one true God, the moral and good Ruler of all things. The gods of the pagans were false.

And more important, the pagans were usually people of low morals. In fact, the worship of the pagans' gods often involved child sacrifice, ritual orgies, and other abominations. So when Judges says, "The Israelites did evil in the eyes of the LORD," we can assume the people's morals were seriously slipping. Fighting the pagans meant not only getting rid of the oppressors, but also getting rid of the influence of people whose religion and morals were corrupting the people of Israel.

We learn in Judges 3 that "the Israelites cried out to the LORD, and he gave them a deliverer—Ehud, a left-handed man" (v. 15). Was it that important, mentioning that he was left-handed? Indeed it was. Read on.

It happened at this stage of history that Israel's oppressor was the nearby nation of Moab, which had formed a coalition with the Ammonites and Amalekites. For eighteen years Moab's king, Eglon, had oppressed Israel. Being under the thumb of Moab meant that Israel had to send Eglon "tribute"—that is, a huge sum of money or goods to appease the oppressor. No tribute meant that slaughter would follow. So Ehud, the left-handed deliverer, went off to Eglon with the tribute payment. Eglon got more than he bargained for.

"Now Ehud had made a double-edged sword about a foot and a half long, which he strapped to his right thigh under his clothing. He presented the tribute to Eglon king of Moab, who was a very fat man" (Judg. 3:16–17). Ehud paid the tribute respectfully, then told Eglon he had a secret message for him. The king sent his own attendants away, and he and

Ehud were alone in the palace. Ehud approached him with the words, "I have a message from God for you" (v. 20).

Eglon was probably expecting something pleasant. Instead, "Ehud reached with his left hand, drew the sword from his right thigh and plunged it into the king's belly. Even the handle sank in after the blade, which came out his back. Ehud did not pull the sword out, and the fat closed in over it" (Judg. 3:21–22).

Note that Ehud's sword was a foot and a half long, so when the account says Eglon was "a very fat man," we know it was so. Note also that Ehud's left-handedness was an advantage: since most men are right-handed, Eglon was not expecting Ehud to draw a sword from his right thigh. Ehud had carried out his sneak attack on the corpulent king beautifully.

He also covered his escape craftily: he locked the door of the room and escaped by another entrance. The servants that had been sent away began to fret over the king, and after a long wait they unlocked the door and found the chubby corpse lying on the floor. Ehud was long gone.

He wasted no time, blowing a trumpet and rallying the men of Israel to rise up and take advantage of the death of Moab's leader. Israel's armies struck down ten thousand Moabites. "And the land had peace for eighty years" (Judg. 3:30). A pleasant ending for a rather gruesome story.

What is admirable about Ehud is not his violence but his shrewdness. He wisely discerned that if Eglon were out of the way, the Moabites would be demoralized, and he devised a brilliant scheme to be alone with the fat oppressor.

God moves in mysterious ways. Most often he does not choose such violent methods to bring about what he desires. But as I said before, these were violent times, and certainly the oppressive King Eglon does not deserve our sympathy.

Honey-Baked Lion, or Lion-Baked Honey

Samson's sweetest moment, and the world's most lethal riddle

We always associate the name *Samson* with the name *Delilah*, the Philistine woman who wheedled from him the secret of his enormous strength. But Delilah was only a mistress, not a wife. Earlier, Samson had married a Philistine woman, which rattled his devout parents. They were shocked that he would pick a wife from among the idol-worshiping, war-making Philistines. We learn in Judges 14 that there was a divine purpose in this attraction: God was using Samson's nearness to the Philistines as a way of getting at those enemies of Israel.

Samson's parents gave in, and on his way to see his lady love, Samson had an encounter to remember: "Suddenly a young lion came roaring toward him. The Spirit of the LORD came upon him in power so that he tore the lion apart with his bare hands as he might have torn a young goat" (Judg. 14:5–6). He went on his way, and sometime later, going back to marry his bride-to-be, he saw the lion again—that is, its carcass, and in it was a swarm of bees and some honey. A man who wasn't afraid of a lion wasn't afraid of bees, naturally. So Samson, not a stickler about table manners, scooped out some honey and ate it as he went along.

We can assume that lion's carcass had been lying there long enough that the vultures and other critters had picked it clean—in other words, it was a lion's skeleton that the bees conveniently used as a hive.

At his wedding banquet, Samson posed a riddle to the Philistine guests. If they could guess the answer, he would provide thirty of them with new sets of clothes. If they failed, they would provide him with thirty sets of clothes. The famous riddle: "Out of the eater, something to eat; / out of the strong, something sweet" (Judg. 14:14).

He gave them one week to answer. After four days they approached his wife (whose name the Bible never mentions) and urged her under threat of death to wheedle the answer out of him. His wife went into a sobbing fit in front of him, which is not an ideal way to spend a honeymoon. Finally he caved in and told her what it meant: it referred to the lion with the honey in it. Specifically, the answer was "What is sweeter than honey? / What is stronger than a lion?" (Judg. 14:18).

Samson was not pleased at losing the bet with the Philistines. Thirty sets of clothes is quite an expense, so he solved his problem in a violent way: he went to the Philistine town of Ashkelon and killed thirty of the men, bringing their clothes to the thirty Philistine guests from the wedding feast. He showed his sneaky wife what he thought of her by returning to live with his parents.

A weird story, as most events in the life of Samson were. The story is even more interesting when you remember that Samson was a Nazirite, meaning he had vowed not to drink wine or touch a dead body. He obviously had to touch the lion's carcass to get the honey out (and Judges 14:6 notes he did not tell his parents about this, for they would have dressed him down for breaking his vow). The banquet he hosted for the Philistines was, according to the Hebrew words, literally a "drinking party," though we aren't told whether he joined his guests in drinking.

Any good moral lessons here? One is that God endows certain people with great power, though most of us will never kill a lion with our bare hands—nor have the opportunity. Another is the matter of the whining wife. She proved by her wheedling the answer to the riddle from him that she wasn't exactly going to be a devoted, supportive wife. Samson had a lot more brawn than brains, but he did one wise thing: he left her and returned home to his folks.

Hot Wheels

A heavenly way to travel

Long before the movie *Chariots of Fire*, there were a couple of prophets who knew a thing or two about such vehicles.

One of these was Elijah, who had quite a few connections with fire. In fact, Elijah is one of the fieriest people in the whole Bible. Things always seemed exciting when he was around. He didn't mince words. He confronted the idol-worshiping king of Israel, Ahab, and Ahab's despicable wife, Jezebel. Ahab's wife had set herself a goal: wipe out the worship of the true God of Israel. She went about the task so thoroughly that most of the true prophets had to hide away in caves. Elijah didn't. He staged a contest: one lone prophet of God versus 450 prophets of the false god Baal.

The famous contest you may already be familiar with; it appears in 1 Kings 18. On Mount Carmel, the herd of Baal prophets staged their religious song and dance, asking Baal to come down from heaven and devour a sacrificed animal. Nothing happened. (Of course it didn't—Baal didn't exist.) Elijah had no need for all the wild shenanigans. He merely called on God once. "Then the fire of the LORD fell, and consumed the burnt offering, and the wood, and the stones, and the dust" (v. 38 RSV). The people of Israel witnessed this wonder, and the message got through to them: Israel's God was real, Baal wasn't, and the Baal prophets were a gang of charlatans.

Elijah, of course, was the true man of God. He was also quite unusual—the Bible never mentions his parents. This is extremely rare. A person is usually "X the son of Y." (It is roughly the equivalent of having a last name.) We don't know who Elijah's father was. It is almost as if the prophet appeared out of nowhere. And if his beginning was mysterious, his ending was both mysterious and spectacular.

According to 2 Kings 2, Elijah did not ever die. He was with his friend and successor, the prophet Elisha, when "a chariot of fire and horses of fire separated the two of them. And Elijah went up by a whirlwind into heaven" (v. 11 RSV).

What is a "chariot of fire"? We don't know for sure. Obviously it appeared to Elisha as bright and burning—which you would expect in a vehicle from heaven. How was it like a "whirlwind"? Again, we don't know. Perhaps the meaning is that it disappeared swiftly. The incident impressed the ancient Jews deeply, for there were many Jewish legends about how Elijah would return to earth as dramatically as he left it. (The incident also impressed American slaves, for it is the source of the old spiritual "Swing Low, Sweet Chariot.")

Elisha himself would have another encounter with chariots of fire. The king of Syria, who had been making war on Israel, sent a mighty army to capture Elisha. (Obviously these people knew prophets had a lot of power.) Elisha's young servant saw the Syrian troops coming and was horror-stricken. Elisha was more confident: "Fear not, for those who are with us are more than those who are with them." Suddenly the servant could see what Elisha saw: "The mountain was full of horses and chariots of fire round about Elisha" (2 Kings 6:16–17 RSV).

Who was riding in those chariots? We don't know. An obvious answer is angels, sent by God to protect his prophet. Apparently the fiery troops didn't have to fight the Syrians, for Elisha himself struck the Syrians with blindness.

The odd story has a happy ending for everyone. Elisha led the blinded Syrians to Israel's king—but instead of killing them (which is what they would expect from an enemy king), he fed them and sent them back to Syria. "And the Syrians came on no more raids into the land of Israel" (2 Kings 16:23 RSV).

Elisha's protector chariots are a reminder that "those who are with us" are far more numerous and more powerful than the enemy. While most of us have never seen the chariots of fire that surround us, they are as real as any human protection, and more reliable.

Curse That Donkey

— ﹘

A beast with more insight than its owner

Many of us grew up laughing at the antics of a talking horse, television's Mister Ed. Ed always seemed wiser and more composed than his human owner, Wilbur. I have always wondered if the scriptwriters for *Mister Ed* might have snitched the concept from the Bible, which presents us with a talking donkey who was wiser than its owner.

The story appears in the book of Numbers. Tucked in between Leviticus and Deuteronomy, Numbers goes unread because people assume it is full of boring laws and rituals, as are the two books around it. Not true. Like Exodus, Numbers is full of action and incident. If you can speed through the first ten chapters (which are pretty dry, frankly), Numbers has some exciting stuff.

Think back to Moses and the Exodus out of Egypt: God had laid ten plagues on Egypt, until finally the stubborn Pharaoh gave in and released the Israelite slaves. Led by Moses, they journeyed slowly—*very* slowly—back to their homeland, Canaan. The journey took forty years—in the Bible's view of things, a whole generation. Along the way there was constant grumbling against God and Moses. Even after witnessing more miracles than most people could even imagine, the people griped. Some talked of returning to Egypt. Moses had to cope with more than one attempted mutiny.

And if the Israelites weren't trouble enough, the lands they passed through were not exactly tolerant of strangers. In those days, a mass migration of people was bad news. They might move in and start killing and looting. The Israelites weren't going to do that, but the nations they passed through were suspicious. They assumed the worst.

Passing through the land of Moab, the horde of Israelites rattled Moab's king, Balak. He expected trouble. (The Amorites had been defeated by the Israelites in battle once, so there was a score to settle.) What to do? Answer: put a curse on them. Specifically, hire a professional prophet to do it.

Balak sent the prophet Balaam a message: "Come now, curse this people for me, since they are too mighty for me; perhaps I shall be able to defeat them and drive them from the land; for I know that he whom you bless is blessed, and he whom you curse is cursed" (Num. 22:6 RSV). The messengers took the message—along with money—to the prophet Balaam. Balaam told the couriers to lodge with him, while he waited to hear a message from God.

The word from God wasn't what Balaam expected: "You shall not curse the people, for they are blessed." So Balaam sent Balak's messengers on their way. Balak sent another group of messengers to the prophet, "more in number and more honorable" than the first group. They dangled more money in front of the prophet, if he would only curse the Israelites. Balaam refused again: "Though Balak were to give me his house full of silver and gold, I could not go beyond the command of the LORD my God" (Num. 22:12, 15, 18 RSV).

But according to Numbers 22:22, Balaam did saddle up his donkey and go to do what Balak asked. "God's anger was kindled because he went; and the angel of the LORD took his stand in the way as his adversary." Riding on his donkey, Balaam did not see the angel "with a drawn sword in his hand"—but the donkey did.

The donkey was no fool—it veered off into a field. Balaam hit the animal, got back on the road, and tried again. The donkey was again frightened by the angel and veered off, causing Balaam to scrape his foot against a wall. Balaam hit the animal again. Passing through a narrow place, the donkey had no place to turn, so it did what donkeys sometimes do: lay down and refused to move. Balaam, furious, struck the beast again.

"Then the LORD opened the mouth of the ass, and she said to Balaam, 'What have I done to you, that you have struck me these three times?'" We can assume Balaam was not accustomed to conversing with a pack animal and must have been shocked. But the Bible doesn't tell us about his facial expression or tone of voice, only his reply to the donkey: "Because you have made sport of me. I wish I had a sword in my hand, for then I would kill you." The donkey's reply is rather touching: "Am I not your ass, upon which you have ridden all your life long to this day? Was I ever accustomed to do so to you?" Balaam's reply: "No" (Num. 22:28–30 RSV).

The story turns rather quickly from amusing and amazing to awesome. Balaam was finally able to see the angel with his drawn sword in the road. He did what people in the Bible often did in the presence of angels: fell down with his face to the ground. (Sometimes angels are comforting, but in some cases their aim is to inspire awe. This one did.)

Balaam had, needless to say, a change of heart and change of plan. Clearly the earlier messages he heard from the Lord were right: he should not curse the Israelites, since God himself had blessed them. Yet on God's order he went to Balak, who assumed the prophet would do as he asked.

Balak eventually took Balaam to a mountain where he could see and curse the thousands of Israelites. Balaam did nothing of the kind: he pronounced a blessing on them—a very long, eloquent blessing, found in Numbers 23–24. He predicted that Israel would be a great nation, one God forever blessed. Balak, the king of Moab, was furious, of course. But Balaam could only answer, "What the LORD speaks, that will I speak" (Num. 24:13 RSV).

What about the talking donkey? Truth? Myth? If you believe in miracles, you can certainly believe that on this one occasion a four-legged pack animal might speak. If you don't, you can still see the meaning of the story: a so-called prophet can be blind to spiritual things (the angel, that is), things even a dumb animal could perceive.

The Bible doesn't tell us any more about Balaam's beast-with-a-voice. We can assume the incident not only made him kinder toward Israel but kinder toward his donkey as well.

The Great Artemis Pep Rally

—

Cheering the lumpy goddess of Ephesus

If you have ever attended a major sports event or a concert held in a huge arena or even a large-scale religious meeting, you understand something basic about human behavior: people occasionally like to gather in large groups and share an experience. There is something about such events that cannot be duplicated. You might enjoy having a few friends over to watch the game on TV, or to enjoy a speaker/singer/actor/preacher. But it is not the same as actually massing together in a specific place and cheering/applauding/shouting/singing together.

The Bible has a few stories of such large-scale gatherings, and one of the most colorful is in Acts 19. Paul, the great missionary preacher of the New Testament, was making a name for himself (and for the gospel) in the Roman province of Asia (the area that today the nation of Turkey occupies). Paul had preached in the major city of Ephesus, and many of the people had converted to the faith. Paul's preaching, as well as the miracles he performed through the power of faith, had made a deep impression. Many of the immoral people of Ephesus had staged a "bonfire of the vanities," burning their occult paraphernalia publicly as a sign they were turning from the false religion to the true.

But if Christianity seized some of the people of Ephesus, fear seized some others. They saw this new religion as a threat to the old religion, which focused on the goddess Artemis. You might recall from your school days that Artemis was one of the many virgin goddesses in Greek mythology. She and her female attendants lived (so the myths said) in the woodlands, hunting with bows and arrows and enjoying their rustic

14

life far from cities (and from men as well). Statues and paintings depicted this goddess as young, beautiful, and chaste.

But this was not the Artemis that the people of Ephesus worshiped. Their Artemis was radically different: a "mother goddess" (there were lots of these in ancient times), the source of the fertility of crops and livestock. This mother goddess of the province of Asia was nothing like the virgin Artemis of most Greek myths, but somehow the name *Artemis* became attached to her anyway. Statues of "Mother Artemis" did not show a young, slender woman but rather a grotesque monster—essentially, a woman's head on a body that was (pardon my bluntness here) covered with breasts. The many breasts were, obviously, symbols of fertility.

It so happened that the city of Ephesus was the center of this Mother Artemis cult. In fact, the city was home to a magnificent building that you'll find listed among the Seven Wonders of the Ancient World, the great Temple of Artemis. Supposedly the temple held an image that fell from heaven. It literally did, for it was a meteorite, and the locals claimed it resembled their own images of the many-breasted goddess.

We learn in Acts 19:24 that the city had a sort of trade union, made up of silversmiths who crafted images of the goddess Artemis. The people of ancient times took their religious bric-a-brac very seriously, and apparently the silversmiths made a good living by selling their Artemis shrines. So Paul and his fellow Christians posed a double threat to these silversmiths. Not only was Christianity a menace to the old-time religion (Artemis worship) but a problem for their pocketbooks as well. So the craftsmen had both economic and religious reasons for hating Christian missionaries.

A ringleader among the silversmiths was a certain Demetrius, who told his fellow craftsmen that Paul taught "that man-made gods are no gods at all." There was the horrible threat that "the goddess herself, who is worshiped throughout the province of Asia and the world, will be robbed of her divine majesty" (Acts 19:26–27).

Demetrius was trying to whip his fellow union members into a frenzy, and he succeeded. They began shouting, "Great is Artemis of the Ephesians!" With a crowd all shouting the same thing, they proceeded to the logical spot: the city's large outdoor amphitheatre.

Crowds, like snowballs, grow as they move along. People inevitably join in just to see what all the ruckus is about. According to Acts, then "the assembly was in confusion: Some were shouting one thing, some another. Most of the people did not even know why they were there." But the lemming mentality took hold of most of them: "They all shouted for about two hours: 'Great is Artemis of the Ephesians!'" (Acts 19:32, 34).

Two hours? Really? Was the author of Acts exaggerating? Probably not. People in ancient times had longer attention spans than we do today. This riot, or pep rally, could very well have lasted two hours, with the participants taking pleasure in sharing their pro-Artemis and anti-Christian ranting and chanting.

The city clerk brought the pep rally to an end by literally reading the people the riot act. He agreed (naturally) with their concern over Artemis and her image "which fell from heaven," but he ordered the people to bring their grievances to court (Acts 19:35, 38).

Did they do so? We never find out. Paul himself did not appear at the riot-rally. (His fellow Christians wisely urged him to stay away from it. Who knows what the frenzied crowd might have done to this man they saw as a serious troublemaker?)

Any lessons to be learned from this odd story? Sure. An obvious one is that people did and still do feel threatened by Christianity. If people become Christian, they put aside their former religion—whether Artemis worship or the secular "me-first" self-worship so popular today. Those who do not convert feel threatened in a spiritual and psychological sense. And there are economic factors as well, for if enough people converted to the faith, what would happen to all the bars, Internet porn sites, strip clubs, casinos, and other morally questionable businesses in this world?

Brimstone Central

—◆—

Those two wicked cities, revisited for the umpteenth time

Thanks to the sex-saturated media, most people over the age of nine probably know what sodomy is. Whether they know the origin of the word is doubtful.

It goes back to Genesis 19, where we learn that Lot, nephew of the righteous man Abraham, lived in the city of Sodom. It was one of five "cities of the plain" (v. 29), and it was notoriously immoral—so bad that in the previous chapter God had told Abraham he intended to destroy it and the nearby city of Gomorrah. Abraham pleaded with God to spare the city, if only for the sake of the few good people who might live there. But it became clear that there were *no* good people there, except for Lot and his family. So God sent two angels to scurry Lot's family out of town before doom came.

Now to the sodomy episode. At night the men of Sodom surrounded Lot's house and demanded he make the visitors available to them—for their sexual pleasure. Lot offered them an alternative—his two virgin daughters—but the Sodomites preferred the male visitors. They became so enraged at Lot that they tried to break down his door.

Lot's two heavenly visitors struck the men of Sodom with blindness. Lot's family fled. Then God poured punishment on the wicked city. "Thus he overthrew those cities and the entire plain, including all those living in the cities—and also the vegetation in the land" (Gen. 19:25). In other words, the whole region was ruined because of the people's wickedness.

The two angels had told Lot's family to flee and "don't look back." Alas, someone did: "Lot's wife looked back, and she became a pillar of salt" (Gen. 19:17, 26).

Did Sodom and the other "cities of the plain" really exist? Definitely. But today "the plain" is probably under the waters of the Dead Sea, perhaps at its southern end. (Incidentally, among the many names the Dead Sea has borne are these two: the Sea of Lot and the Sodomitish Sea.) The land in that area is dry and covered with salt deposits. Lot's wife, who disobeyed God, looked back on Sodom and turned into a pillar of salt; she would have fit in perfectly with the scenery.

What about the destruction of the cities? The King James Version says God sent "brimstone and fire" (Gen. 19:24). Modern versions have fire and "burning sulfur." Sounds like a volcano, doesn't it? It is quite possible God used a volcanic eruption to destroy the immoral towns.

The old story is full of all kinds of life lessons. One Jesus himself expressed: "Remember Lot's wife" (Luke 17:32). We all should remember Lot's wife. Aside from disobeying a direct command from God, she had all-bad reasons for looking back: sentiment, curiosity, the fear she had left something behind and wanted to go back and get it.

The Bible tells us the cities were notoriously wicked. It doesn't tell us exactly what their wickedness consisted of, though we do know the local men were attempting homosexual rape. Even after all these centuries, the names *Sodom* and *Gomorrah* still conjure up images of vice and depravity. TV, movies, and pop music have so conditioned us to tolerate vice that we need to reread Genesis 19 now and then, reminding ourselves that God takes sin very seriously.

Wormy Herod

Pride goeth before destruction

There are several men in the New Testament named Herod, and they are all rather nasty characters. The first is that vile ruler associated with the birth of Jesus, the man known to history as (ironically) Herod the Great. He was "great" only in the sense that he did create some impressive buildings (including a lavish remodeling of the temple in Jerusalem). He was not great in a moral sense. You might recall that when the wise men came to seek out the infant Jesus, the malicious Herod ordered the slaughter of the male infants of Bethlehem.

Herod the Great's descendants followed in the old man's tradition of malice and immorality. One of these was Herod Agrippa I, grandson of Herod the Great. This younger Herod had grown up in Rome as the friend of a young man who eventually became the vicious emperor Caligula. The emperor bestowed the title *king* on Herod Agrippa and allowed him to rule over the lands of his deposed uncle, the Herod that Jesus encountered before his crucifixion. (Alas, the New Testament does not help us keep track of these men, since it simply calls them all "Herod," and they were three different people.) After Caligula's death, the Roman emperor Claudius extended Herod Agrippa's territory to include the province of Judea, which included Jerusalem.

The Jews generally despised members of the Herod family, but they rather liked Herod Agrippa I. He decided he liked being liked, and he did what he could to make the Jews happy. He found that one way of doing this was to persecute that new group known as Christians. So he had James, one of the original twelve apostles, executed by beheading with a sword (Acts 12:2), thus making James the first martyr among the apostles.

19

Herod saw that this pleased the Jewish religious authorities in Jerusalem, so he sought to please them further by throwing Peter in prison. Acts 12:5–16 tells of Peter's dramatic rescue from prison. The night before he was to be tried before Herod, Peter was asleep between two guards, bound to them with chains. An angel from God appeared and miraculously freed Peter. Peter, thinking he was dreaming or having a vision, found himself walking without harm by the various guards. When Peter appeared at the home of his Christian brothers, they were shocked. They had been praying for his release but were awestruck when it actually happened.

Herod was (to put it mildly) not pleased that this leader among the troublesome Christians had somehow escaped. It clearly did not occur to him that God might have performed a miracle, so he assumed the obvious: the stupid, incompetent guards were to blame. So he had them executed (Acts 12:19). You have to pity these poor men: they fell asleep with this prisoner chained to them and awoke to find him gone—with the wrath of Herod awaiting them.

Powerful and violent men do not always get their punishment in this world, but on occasion they do, as Acts 12:20–23 shows us. The king had gone to the city of Caesarea and was holding an official audience. The powerful did and do like to make a big impression at such times, so on this occasion Herod Agrippa was dressed to kill—or be killed. Acts tells us he was "wearing his royal robes" and was sitting on his throne, and we can assume the people present were quite dazzled. We aren't told what he said in his official speech, but he made a definite impression, for the people there shouted, "This is the voice of a god, not of a man" (Acts 12:21–22).

The vain Herod must have been mightily pleased at this, but he was not pleased for long: "Because Herod did not give praise to God, an angel of the Lord struck him down, and he was eaten by worms and died." The account follows with these words: "But the word of God continued to increase and spread" (Acts 12:23–24). Interesting: the vain, proud persecutor of Christians fell dead, while the faith he persecuted continued to spread.

The Jewish historian Josephus also told the brief story in Acts, and he threw in some more details. Herod's royal robes were made of some kind of silver cloth, which glittered splendidly in the sunlight. Josephus, a good Jew, took the same view that Christians did: Herod had no business accepting the people's praise of him as "a god." Josephus claims Herod was seized with a severe pain in his abdomen, bringing on a violent attack that resulted in his death. This is one of the occasions when the events related in the Bible match perfectly with what the historians wrote down.

Except for one detail, that is: Josephus makes no mention of the "angel of the Lord" striking Herod down; Acts does. Meaning what? That the Acts account depicts a white-robed winged messenger coming down upon Herod? Not necessarily. In the Bible, God's angels sometimes appear like human beings, and sometimes do not appear visibly at all. The author of Acts was making a valid point: divine power had struck down the proud Herod. Josephus would not have disagreed.

God does not always intervene so dramatically in the world's affairs. Sometimes he thwarts cruel, proud persecutors (as he did Herod), and some he allows to die quietly in their old age (think of Stalin and Mao). Whatever their fate in this world, the message of Acts 12 is the same: the truth continues to spread, while the pomp and cruelty of earthly powers pass away.

The Ark, Pre-Hollywood

Israel's sacred box and a fishy pagan god

Very likely you have seen the movie *Raiders of the Lost Ark*, which was about a modern quest for the ark of the covenant. The ark depicted in the movie actually does fit the description found in the Bible (see Exod. 25:10–22). It was a gold-covered wooden chest (*ark* simply means "chest" or "box"), carried on two poles by four men. Its solid-gold lid had images of two winged creatures (the cherubim) facing each other, the tips of their wings touching. Inside the ark were the stone tablets inscribed with the Ten Commandments.

The ark signified God's presence among the Israelites. They did not actually worship the ark (since the Ten Commandments forbade worshiping anything but God himself), but they did consider it sacred. The ark was the centerpiece of the tabernacle, the large tent where Moses went to meet with God.

Because the ark symbolized God's presence, the Israelites associated miracles with it—such as crossing the Jordan River on dry land and the crumbling of the walls of Jericho (Josh. 3, 6).

The movie would have you believe that protector spirits guarded the ark. Mostly this was an excuse for the Hollywood special effects whiz kids to impress audiences with some pretty frightening images. It is definitely true, however, that the Israelites believed that God's power was somehow connected with the ark. And so, inevitably, as Israel warred with its various neighbors, those neighbor nations hoped to capture the ark. On one occasion they did, much to their regret.

It was the warlike Philistines who captured the ark. They were people who inhabited the Mediterranean coast west of Israel. The Old Testament makes it clear that the Israelites and Philistines despised each other. Apparently the Philistines did not practice circumcision, for the Old Testament sometimes refers to the Philistines as "the uncircumcised." They did not worship Israel's God but had gods of their own, including a fish-shaped god named Dagon.

His name actually means "fish," and perhaps it was appropriate that a coastal people would have such a god. We aren't certain, but it appears likely that Dagon was depicted as a sort of "mer-man"—half-man, half-fish. You might recall that in Judges 16, the strongman Samson's last act was to tear down the temple of Dagon.

In 1 Samuel 5 you can read about what befell the Philistines when they captured the ark and took it to their city of Ashdod. Naturally they deposited it in the temple of Dagon—a way of proclaiming, "Our god triumphed over your God!" But in the morning they found the statue of Dagon fallen flat on its face before the ark. They set the statue back where it was, but the next morning found it on its face again—and this time with his head and hands broken off.

Then worse things happened: "The LORD's hand was heavy upon the people of Ashdod and its vicinity; he brought devastation upon them and afflicted them with tumors" (1 Sam. 5:6).

The Philistines were sharp enough to see that the ark was giving them trouble, so they moved it to their city of Gath—where, again, it brought disease upon the people. They moved it to another city, and the same thing happened. After seven months of trouble after capturing the ark, the Philistines finally wised up and sent it back to Israel, along with a gold "guilt offering" (1 Sam. 6:3) as a way of pacifying this very powerful God of Israel. Clearly God could be very protective toward the ark of the covenant, a message that was driven home not only to the Philistines but to Israel as well.

When King David made Jerusalem his capital city, he brought the ark there. During the reign of his son Solomon, the ark's permanent resting place was the great temple that Solomon built (1 Kings 8).

What became of the ark? No one really knows. The movie *Raiders of the Lost Ark* was correct in claiming that it had mysteriously disappeared. Very likely it was captured when the Babylonians destroyed the temple in 586 B.C. The Apocrypha contains the legend that the prophet Jeremiah hid the ark away in a cave somewhere (2 Macc. 2:5). Probably some conquering empire long ago stripped it of its gold because they regarded it as nothing more than an empty box, suitable for firewood. But while the ark existed in Israel, the people honored it, and so did the pagan Philistines who had the misfortune of bringing the ark into their own territory.

Any moral lesson to be learned from the story of the ark? It might be helpful to recall what the ark symbolized: God's presence. The ark was a reminder to the Israelites that God was actually there among them—not far off in the sky somewhere. But the power associated with the ark reminded them of something else: God was awesome. The ark was no ordinary wooden chest, a piece of household furniture. In fact, human hands could not touch it, and they had always to carry it on two poles.

So the message was this: God is here among us, but he is powerful and we must treat him with reverence and respect. The ark no longer exists, but the ideas connected with it are still valid.

The Child-Eating Hell God

—

Oh, the things people will worship . . .

Ever wonder why the Bible pictures hell as a place of fire? Blame it on the worship of a bloodthirsty god named Molech. His name means "king," and he was the supreme god of the Ammonites, a neighbor nation of Israel. In some of their worship sites, the Ammonites heated an image of Molech like a furnace, then placed slaughtered infants in its arms and burned them. This gruesome sacrifice was accompanied by cymbals and other noises—no doubt to drown out the children's pitiful screams.

Most people of ancient Israel—its prophets especially—were appalled at child sacrifice, even though it was fairly common in the world in those days. Some Israelites fell into worshiping the god Molech, and even some of Israel's kings, including the wise Solomon, set up worship sites for Molech. The wicked king Manasseh sacrificed his own son to Molech (2 Kings 21:6). The prophets of Israel spoke out boldly against Israelites who were so spiritually callous that they could participate in worshiping Molech, then turn and worship at the temple of God (see Jer. 7:9–11, Ezek. 23:37–39).

True, Israel's God required people to sacrifice animals to him. But sacrifice of humans—and innocent babies in particular—was never a part of Israel's religion. While today we think of animal sacrifice as pretty primitive, the Israelites were more compassionate than their neighbors, for they certainly never sacrificed humans to God. How, the prophets of Israel wondered, could any people bow down to an image of a god so horrible that he desired the death of children? Such a god was nothing like the true God, the good and wise Ruler of Israel. In fact,

25

gods like Molech, gods pleased with the senseless loss of human life, were not gods at all, but demons.

If you ever read John Milton's epic poem *Paradise Lost*, you might recall that Molech is a character in it. The poem tells the familiar story of Adam and Eve and their temptation, and Satan and his fellow demons are also present. Milton followed the tradition that the pagan gods of ancient times were actually demons, and so Molech is part of the group, along with various other pagan gods mentioned in the Bible. Milton refers to Molech as the "grisly king," a reminder that the name *Molech* actually meant "king." Milton probably wondered, as we would wonder today, what sort of people would give the title "king" to a god who required them to slaughter their own infants.

The Valley of Ben Hinnom outside Jerusalem was notorious as a slaughter site, a place where people sacrificed children to the god Molech. The good king Josiah put a stop to these abominations, but for years people remembered the site as a place of idol worship and death. In the period between the Old and New Testaments, some Jewish writers claimed Ben Hinnom was the gateway to hell. The Hebrew name *Ben Hinnom* passed into Greek as *Gehenna*, and in the Greek New Testament, *Gehenna* signified the place of eternal punishment—translated in our English Bibles as "hell," naturally.

Jesus himself used the word several times. To him, and to everyone else who used the word, *Gehenna* brought to mind the sacrificial fires of the gruesome god Molech. Also, years after the ending of these terrible sacrifices, the site was used as Jerusalem's garbage dump and was kept continually burning. Into it people threw not just household garbage but also animal carcasses and the bodies of executed criminals. This was King Josiah's idea: he knew if he turned the site into a garbage dump, Molech's worshipers would no longer wish to conduct their horrible rituals there. No wonder Gehenna indicated a loathsome place of unending fire.

Gehenna was sometimes referred to by another name, *Topheth*. The name may mean "fire place" or "place to be spit upon." Or it may come from the word *toph*, meaning "drum." As I mentioned, worshipers used drums, cymbals, and other noisemakers during the sacrifice of infants to drown out their wails. As with Gehenna, the name *Topheth* came to be used as a synonym for hell (see Isa. 30:33, Jer. 7:31).

The worship of Molech is a painful reminder that human beings will not only tolerate evil and practice evil, but even go so far as to bow down to it. Maybe this is rooted in a basic human fear that evil is really more powerful than good. But the whole Bible reminds us that evil is destined for destruction.

Raising Cain a Wife

The first outlaw, and that woman from who-knows-where

You've heard the expression "raising Cain," but did you know the origin of it? It was a polite way of saying "raising hell." Cain, the world's first murderer and first outlaw, was assumed to be in hell, so instead of saying "raising hell," people substituted "raising the devil" or "raising Cain."

Cain and Abel were, as you probably know, the first two sons of Adam and Eve. You probably also know that Cain killed Abel, and we don't list that here as a bizarre occurrence because, sadly, murder itself is neither bizarre nor weird in this fallen world. But after Abel's death, there are some other bizarre items connected with Cain, notably the matter of his spouse.

Cain killed Abel in a field, with no witnesses—except God, that is. God put a curse on Cain, condemning him to be a "restless wander on the earth" (Gen. 4:14). Cain had been a farmer, but under the curse, the ground would never yield food for him again. Cain cried out to God that anyone who found him would kill him. And now you are scratching your head, asking, "Who else was there on earth then, except his own parents?"

Obviously there was someone else, for "Cain went out from the LORD's presence and lived in the land of Nod, east of Eden. Cain lay with his wife, and she became pregnant and gave birth to Enoch" (Gen. 4:16–17).

That other question—*Where did Cain get his wife?*—has puzzled readers for centuries. If you think we can settle the matter here, sorry. Clearly he married a woman, and she either had to be one of his own sisters, or there were other people on earth besides Adam's family. Neither answer is really satisfactory. And neither is the old Jewish legend that Adam had a wife besides Eve—meaning that Cain's wife would have been his half-sister instead of sister.

One suggestion has been that Adam was not the only human ancestor. There were others, but only a descendant of Adam survived the flood (Noah, that is), so Genesis focuses on Adam as the ancestor of Noah and his sons, who were the "starter families" after the flood wiped out all other people on earth. An interesting solution, one that won't satisfy most people—but then, neither do the other answers.

Genesis tells us that Adam had many sons and daughters after the birth of his son Seth. Noah and his sons were descendants of Seth—meaning all the rest of us are, too. Cain's progeny were all wiped out at the flood. After Genesis 4, the Bible never mentions Cain again, except for a few places in the New Testament that hold him up as an example of a wicked man.

The story of Cain taking a wife doesn't offer much of a moral lesson. It does teach one valuable idea, though: do not get bogged down in these questions. Focus on the parts of the Bible that are clear—such as "love your neighbor as yourself" and "love God with all your heart."

Moses' Snakebite Cure

The magic a bronze snake can do

If you have seen the movie *The Ten Commandments*, you probably recall that after Moses led the Israelite slaves out of Egypt, he had to face constant complaining. Yes, they were no longer slaves working for the Egyptians, and yes, they were on their way to their ancestral home in Canaan. But they griped almost constantly, mostly because the route from Egypt to Canaan was an ugly wilderness providing little food or water. Chalk it up to human nature: we prefer the devil we know to the devil we don't know. Things were bad in Egypt, true, but after all, they did have plenty of food to eat there . . .

Well, needless to say, if they had turned around and gone back to Egypt, their former masters would not have welcomed them with open arms. They might very well have killed the Israelites, or taken them into slavery again. More important, it wasn't God's will for them to remain in Egypt. They were to get to Canaan—in God's own good time—and become the chosen nation of Israel. But in the meantime, they groused, and Moses had to hear and bear their grievances.

That brings us to the book of Numbers, an interesting but neglected part of the Old Testament. Readers find they enjoy Exodus, with its exciting story of Moses, Pharaoh, the plagues on Egypt, the parting of the Red Sea, the giving of the Law on Mount Sinai. But readers quickly get bored with Leviticus and its pages of endless rules and rituals. Too bad they don't press on to Numbers, for it continues the Exodus story, with the Israelites passing through hostile territories, fighting pagan foes, and more often, grumbling against the patient Moses.

Numbers reports this curious incident when some major griping drew a major punishment:

> Then the LORD sent venomous snakes among them; they bit the people and many Israelites died. The people came to Moses and said, "We sinned when we spoke against the LORD and against you. Pray that the LORD will take the snakes away from us." So Moses prayed for the people.
>
> The LORD said to Moses, "Make a snake and put it up on a pole; anyone who is bitten can look at it and live." So Moses made a bronze snake and put it up on a pole. Then when anyone was bitten by a snake and looked at the bronze snake, he lived. (Num. 21:6–9)

The story seems to be referring to venomous snakes, which raises an obvious question: how the heck could people bitten by venomous snakes be healed by looking at a metal snake on a pole? There is no scientific explanation, though if you are prepared to accept a supernatural explanation, you can say it was a miracle.

Some Bible scholars think there really was a scientific explanation. The Hebrew words that we translate as "venomous snakes" literally mean "fiery snakes." That could mean snakes that were poison, true, but it might also be referring to a nasty creature called a Guinea worm—not a snake at all, but a wormlike parasite that burrows under the skin and causes burning pain in the body. A person extracts the Guinea worm (which can be as long as three feet) by cutting a gash in the skin near the worm's head (or tail) and carefully winding it around an object, such as a stick. The process may take days, until finally the entire worm is out. Done too quickly, the worm breaks off, with part of it still inside the human body.

This is probably more scientific detail than you wanted to hear, but even today natives of the Middle East and the tropical parts of India and Africa treat the Guinea-worm infection with the wrap-it-around-the-stick method. It is entirely possible that the Israelites in the wilderness drank water polluted with the larvae of the Guinea worms, and that this happened right after one of their many "gripe rebellions" against Moses.

How Moses came to know of the stick cure is open to question. Perhaps one of the Israelites knew of the cure; perhaps God himself revealed it to Moses. At any rate, scholars who believe that the "fiery serpents" were really Guinea worms believe that the bronze snake on the pole may have been a sort of visual aid, Moses' reminder to the people that the way of curing the sickness was to wind the "serpent" (worm, that is) around a stick.

Anyhow, the bronze snake method worked. We hear no more of it until hundreds of years later, during the reign of King Hezekiah of Israel. Hezekiah, like all the good kings, did what he could to rid Israel of idol worship. It turns out that one of the idols the people were worshiping was the bronze snake from the days of Moses. The snake even had a name: Nehushtan (see 2 Kings 18:1–4). The Israelites had been burning incense to it—meaning they had probably forgotten its original purpose and simply looked upon it as a snake idol, something else to worship.

Though he probably had a deep respect for Moses, Hezekiah had the bronze snake destroyed. Certainly Moses would have approved, for one of the Ten Commandments strictly forbade worshiping any kind of image.

The bronze snake was mentioned again, and by Jesus himself. "Just as Moses lifted up the snake in the desert, so the Son of Man must be lifted up, that everyone who believes in him may have eternal life" (John 3:14). "Son of Man" was the name Jesus often used to refer to himself. He was announcing that his death and resurrection (being "lifted up") would heal people, just as the bronze snake served to heal the Israelites in the wilderness.

The difference was, of course, that the healing the bronze snake caused was only temporary, while the spiritual healing Jesus' death and resurrection brought about would have eternal consequences. Moses' bronze snake, lifted up on a pole, saved people from physical death, and Jesus, lifted up on a cross, saved people from eternal death.

The One and Only
Original Scapegoat

Hoofing it under a load of sins

You hear this word used all the time, and it refers to someone who takes the blame for someone else—the same meaning as the more modern term *fall guy*. In the original sense, more than three thousand years ago, a scapegoat was a real goat. On the annual Day of Atonement, Israel's high priest would lay his hands on a goat, symbolically transferring the people's sins to it. Then the creature would be driven away into the wilderness. The scapegoat fared better than the other Day of Atonement goat, which the priest sacrificed as a sin offering.

You'll find all this in Leviticus:

> He [the high priest] is to cast lots for the two goats—one lot for the LORD and the other for the scapegoat. Aaron shall bring the goat whose lot falls to the LORD and sacrifice it for a sin offering. But the goat chosen by lot as the scapegoat shall be presented alive before the LORD to be used for making atonement by sending it into the desert as a scapegoat . . .
>
> The man who releases the goat as a scapegoat must wash his clothes and bathe himself with water; afterward he may come into the camp. (Lev. 16:8–10, 26)

You may already know that the Jews took—and take—the Day of Atonement very seriously. The purpose of this holy day was to remind people of the collective sins of the whole year. On this day the high priest made confession for all the people's sins and entered into the innermost part of the temple, the Holy of Holies, where he sprinkled blood on the ark of the covenant. The solemn day involved godly sorrow over sin, but also rejoicing over God's forgiveness.

The emphasis on sin offends modern sensibilities, and so does all the business about sacrifice and blood. But the key idea behind sacrifice and atonement is that human sin offends a holy God, so something must occur to bring about a reconciliation between man and God. Israel, like most nations, practiced animal sacrifices. These strike us as cruel, but when you consider that some cultures sacrificed humans, animal sacrifice does seem more progressive. A major change occurred among the early Christians, who believed the old system of animal sacrifices had been done away with forever because Christ himself became the final, once-and-for-all sacrifice for human sin.

Now, back to our four-footed friend, the scapegoat. The passage referring to this goat gives Bible translators fits. The word translated "scapegoat" is the Hebrew *azazel*. No one is 100 percent sure what it means. The probable meaning is "goat that goes away" (that is, into the wilderness). English Bible translator William Tyndale in the 1500s came up with the term "scapegoat," and most English Bibles still use this. But *azazel* might also mean "desolate region" or even "demon of the wilderness." Some scholars think this is the real meaning of *azazel* in Leviticus 16: one goat was the Lord's (for the sin offering) and one was for the wilderness demon (the goat driven into the desert).

Curiously, in Hebrew legends, Azazel was the name of a demon, one who seduced people into doing evil. This demon of desert places was thought of as hideously ugly, with seven serpent heads and batlike wings. Folk tales say he taught men aggression by teaching them to make swords, and he taught women vanity by giving them cosmetics. Azazel was also an alternate name for Satan himself.

Whatever the correct translation of *azazel* might be, the basic idea remains: once a year a goat was driven off into the wilderness, symbolically bearing the people's sins far away from them. If you ever want to see a vivid image of this creature, log on to an Internet search engine and type in "Holman Hunt scapegoat." That should take you to a website where you can view Holman Hunt's famous painting *The Scapegoat*.

By the way, if the practice of sending a goat off into the wilderness sounds mean-spirited to you, take heart: goats are among the hardiest animals the Lord ever created, with an appetite for whatever food is available. The scapegoat munching on some desert weed was probably very thankful that it had not suffered the fate of the other goat, the one sacrificed as a sin offering.

The ritual of the scapegoat reminds us of something we so easily forget in the modern "no-fault" world: sin is serious. It needs to be "done away with," as the driving away of the goat made clear.

Sons of God, Human Beauties—and Fallen Giants

Those mysterious pre-Flood inhabitants of earth

You have no doubt heard the phrase *fallen angel*, right? How about *fallen giants?* In a very short passage of Genesis 6, we meet fallen giants and all sorts of mysterious beings.

"When men began to increase in number on the earth and daughters were born to them, the sons of God saw that the daughters of men were beautiful, and they married any of them they chose" (Gen. 6:1–2). Understand any of that? After many centuries, the scholars aren't sure what it all means. Many say the "sons of God" were angels, but the Bible certainly gives no hint that angels could marry human beings. It makes more sense that the "sons of God" were godly men, who married beautiful (but not godly) women. (Note that the women are not called "daughters of God.")

Another theory: the "sons of God" were kings, the bigwigs in a primitive warrior society, who took beautiful women into their harems. Pick any theory you like, for none of them will ever be accepted by everyone.

Now, another puzzling group: "The Nephilim were on the earth in those days—and also afterward—when the sons of God went to the daughters of men and had children by them. They were the heroes of old, men of renown" (Gen. 6:4). The Hebrew word *Nephilim* means "fallen ones," and it reoccurs in Numbers 13, referring to giant men. It may simply be referring to very large-framed, powerful men, not to any kind of supernatural being.

Did the author of Genesis believe (or know) that there had been giants existing on the earth? There were giants in Greek mythology, who existed before the normal-sized humans took over the earth, and there are giants in other world mythologies. Maybe all those mythologies share a common foundation in what really happened ages ago. In the Greek mythology, the giants were bad, and these Nephilim (judging from their name "fallen ones") were also bad. And one further connection with mythology: Genesis 6:4 speaks of the "heroes of old, men of renown"—the sort of larger-than-life heroes that populate the Greek epics, men such as Achilles, Hector, Hercules, and Perseus. Perhaps such amazing people really did exist "once upon a time."

When did they exist? We don't know, for the passage is sandwiched in between a long genealogy, then follows the account of Noah and the Flood. We are probably meant to connect these "sons of God" and the Nephilim and the heroes with what follows, the announcement that "The LORD saw how great man's wickedness on the earth had become, and that every inclination of the thoughts of his heart was only evil all the time" (Gen. 6:5). Apparently the "heroes of old" were renowned, but not because they had good morals. As in the Greek mythology, the "heroes" were powerful and could do impressive feats, but God saw them for what they were: selfish and wicked.

And that, needless to say, is probably the chief moral lesson of this puzzling passage. Genesis matter-of-factly refers to the "heroes of old, men of renown," but does not praise them, then immediately announces that the Lord was displeased at man's wickedness. Lesson understood: mankind has often set up "heroes" who were not decent human beings. We need only cast a glance around at our present society and see that the age of Genesis 6 may not be so different from our own.

Moses the Mountain Goat

—

Israel's greatest leader ... with horns?

One of the greatest artists of all time was the Italian genius Michelangelo, and one of his most famous works was his statue of Moses. You have probably seen pictures of it, an awesome marble image of the man of God, muscular and bearded, holding the stone tablets with the Ten Commandments carved on them. And on top of Moses' head are . . . two horns. Ever wonder about those? Many people have. There is an old Sunday school joke about the child who asked his teacher about the picture of Moses with two horns of his head. The teacher replied, "He stayed so long on Mount Sinai that he turned into a mountain goat." Silly answer, and not the right one. So where did those horns come from?

Let's remember the importance of Moses. He is the most significant character in the Old Testament, the deliverer of the Israelites from Egypt, the man who communicated God's divine Law to the people. Exodus through Deuteronomy tells his story (and Genesis through Deuteronomy are traditionally called the "five books of Moses"). Exodus relates that the Egyptian pharaoh tried to exterminate all the sons of the Israelite slaves living in Egypt. Moses' mother and sister placed the infant Moses in a basket in the river, where Pharaoh's daughter found him and raised him at Egypt's court. Moses could have led a luxurious royal life, but after killing an Egyptian official for abusing a Hebrew slave, Moses fled. He first encountered God in the famous burning bush story (Exod. 3).

And that fateful encounter set a pattern for Moses' life: he was the one person who could literally *see* God. "The LORD would speak to Moses face to face, as a man speaks with his friend" (Exod. 33:11). "No prophet has risen in Israel like Moses, whom the LORD knew face to face"

(Deut. 34:10). All the Israelites were God's chosen people—but Moses was somehow special, the man who could, in some mysterious way, get up close to the awesome invisible God of Israel.

Exodus relates that Moses made a request of God: "Now show me your glory."

> And the LORD said, "I will cause all my goodness to pass in front of you, and I will proclaim my name, the LORD, in your presence . . . But," he said, "you cannot see my face, for no one may see me and live."
>
> Then the LORD said, "There is a place near me where you may stand on a rock. When my glory passes by, I will put you in a cleft in the rock and cover you with my hand until I have passed by. Then I will remove my hand and you will see my back; but my face must not be seen." (Exod. 33:18–23)

What did Moses see on that occasion? We would all love to know that. In some mysterious sense Moses "saw God," yet Exodus is using human terms—"back," "face," "hand"—to describe something quite indescribable. Moses' fellow Israelites had witnessed the pillar of fire and pillar of cloud that God used to guide them through the wilderness. But somehow Moses himself experienced God "as a man speaks with his friend."

Following this dramatic encounter, Moses carved out a new set of the Ten Commandments on stone tablets. He had "seen" God and had written down the commandments of God. We would somehow expect him to be changed by this meeting, and indeed he was:

> When Moses came down from Mount Sinai with the two tablets of the Testimony in his hands, he was not aware that his face was radiant because he had spoken with the LORD. When Aaron and all the Israelites saw Moses, his face was radiant, and they were afraid to come near him. But Moses called to them; so Aaron and all the leaders of the community came back to him, and he spoke to them. Afterward all the Israelites came near him, and he gave them all the commands the LORD had given him on Mount Sinai.
>
> When Moses finished speaking to them, he put a veil over his face. But whenever he entered the LORD's presence to speak with him, he removed the veil until he came out. And when he came out and told the

Israelites what he had been commanded, they saw that his face was radiant. Then Moses would put the veil back over his face until he went in to speak with the LORD. (Exod. 34:29–35)

In short, Moses literally beamed after his meeting with God. The glow was so otherworldly and frightening that he had to hide it under a veil. But note that he took the veil off again when he entered God's presence—after all, God was so glorious himself that he would not, like the Israelites, be intimidated by the glow of Moses.

Now, back to those horns: the Hebrew words that we translate as "glowing" or "radiant" are related to the Hebrew word for "horn." Around the year 400, the Bible scholar Jerome, translating the Old Testament from Hebrew into Latin, made a slight error: he used the Latin word for "horns" in this passage, and so for several centuries readers of the Latin Bible got the impression that Moses did indeed come down from Mount Sinai with horns projecting from his face. Michelangelo was one of many artists who depicted a horned Moses. Happily, our Bible translations today are more accurate in describing the "radiant" or "glowing" face of Moses.

What are we to make of the story of Moses on the mountain? You can call it a legend, or you can assume that if a man really did meet with God, as Moses did, that he would be dramatically changed in some way—perhaps in his face, and certainly on the inside as well.

The Maltese Viper

O, ye fickle, superstitious pagans

One of the pleasures in reading the book of Acts in the New Testament is that parts of it are firsthand accounts. Luke, who wrote the third Gospel, wrote the entire book of Acts. In much of Acts he was simply reporting what others told him about the early years of Christianity. But parts of the book are called the "we sections," sections where it is obvious that Luke himself was actually present. These sections impress readers with their vividness and details. Luke was telling his readers, "I was there when this happened."

One of the most vivid of all the "we sections" appears in chapters 27 and 28. The great apostle Paul was on his way to Rome to stand trial before the Roman emperor. Since Luke was there also, we must assume some of Paul's Christian brothers were allowed to accompany the prisoner. Acts 27:13–44 describes an awesome storm at sea, one so frightening that some of the crew members tried to save their own necks by escaping in a lifeboat. The storm was so fierce, and the 276 people on board so terrified, that they threw overboard everything they could think of. "When neither sun nor stars appeared for many days and the storm continued raging, we finally gave up all hope of being saved" (Acts 27:20).

Paul was not disheartened. He told his fellow travelers that God had sent an angel to reassure him that he would arrive safely in Rome. But this didn't necessarily mean that the ship would follow its regular route. As Paul predicted, the ship would run aground on an island.

The island happened to be Malta, or Melita, as it was sometimes called. The name was appropriate, for it was an old Canaanite word meaning "refuge." We can well imagine the storm-tossed travelers' relief

41

at finally setting foot on land after such an ordeal. Not only were they on solid earth again, but "the islanders showed us unusual kindness" (Acts 28:2). Though it was raining and cold, the locals built a fire and welcomed the refugees from the storm.

Paul was technically a prisoner, but that didn't mean he sat idly by, pouting at being in the custody of a Roman soldier. Being the compassionate soul that he was, he did what some of the others did: gathered up more wood for the fire. Everyone who has ever gathered up wood—either from one's home woodpile or from the forest floor—knows that snakes and other nasty creatures like to hide under wood. Apparently Paul or someone else had managed to pick up a snake along with the wood and naturally, when thrown on the fire, the snake made a swift and angry exit. It bit Paul on the hand and held on.

Suddenly the friendly islanders showed how superstitious they were. "This man must be a murderer; for though he escaped from the sea, Justice has not allowed him to live" (Acts 28:4). Pagans jumped easily to such conclusions, and they would not have understood our "scientific" explanation for what happened—namely, a snake happened to be in the wood, and it bit Paul because he happened to be nearby.

They were wrong about divine Justice: "Paul shook the snake off into the fire and suffered no ill effects. The people expected him to swell up or suddenly fall dead, but after waiting a long time and seeing nothing unusual happen to him, they changed their minds and said he was a god" (Acts 28:5–6).

Luke's account of the incident says the snake was a "viper," meaning it was venomous. There are no poisonous snakes on Malta today (so the biologists tell us), but there might have been some there two thousand years ago. Surely the local people who expected Paul to suffer from the snakebite must have been familiar with their own local snakes.

Why wasn't Paul affected? A miracle? Perhaps, though Acts doesn't give any hint that this was the case. Venomous snakes are sometimes temporarily harmless because they have used up their supply of poison for the moment. Luke, who was present at the scene, seems more interested in how the local people reacted: they changed their attitude quickly, from believing Paul was cursed by the gods to believing he was a god himself. Luke, a former pagan himself, sometimes seems to be poking fun at how superstitious the pagans were.

But Paul's survival, having made an impression on the locals, was a kind of preparation for what followed: he performed several miraculous cures on the island, and the Maltese "honored us in many ways" (Acts 28:10). Much more impressive than surviving the bite of the viper were the miracles of compassion Paul did among the people. Just as Jesus cured the sick, so did the first generation of his disciples. It might surprise many skeptics—and even many Christians—that healings and other miracles still occur among people of faith.

Dancing for Fun and Prophet

A human head—the perfect gift for a dancing daughter

In the Bible, the saints don't always live long and prosper in this world. One of the classic examples is Jesus' kinsman, the righteous wilderness prophet known as John the Baptist. One of the Bible's most bizarre stories concerns how he met an untimely end because a lecherous middle-aged politician lusted after his own stepdaughter.

The politician was the unscrupulous Herod, whose wife, named Herodias, had been married to Herod's own brother, Philip. (You can already tell this was not a spiritually healthy family.) Matthew 14 tells us that Herodias divorced Philip and married Herod, a violation of Jewish law.

John, who feared God but no human, no matter how powerful, spoke out against this unlawful divorce, and no doubt John was aware that the Herod family was notoriously immoral in just about every way. Herodias despised John for calling her and Herod adulterers, and she persuaded Herod to throw the prophet in prison. Herod was somewhat religious—or more accurately, superstitious—and was actually afraid to have John killed, partly because he knew the Jews honored John, partly because he himself wondered if John might be a true prophet.

At a birthday banquet for Herod, Herodias's daughter by her first marriage danced for the partiers. We aren't told the girl's name, though secular histories tell us it was Salome. Whether she danced the "dance of the seven veils," as tradition says, is not known. Apparently the dance, whatever it was, pleased (and titillated) her randy stepfather. Under her influence, and probably under the influence of wine also, Herod made a rash promise: because of her dance, she could have anything she wished.

He probably expected her to ask for jewels or clothing or such. But her mother took her aside and made another suggestion, and not one Herod expected: the head of John the Baptist on a platter. Herod could not have been pleased at this, but he had made a solemn vow in front of his guests. So, to save his own face, he took John's head. He had John beheaded immediately, and the proof brought in for all to see. Dutifully, the girl took it to her mother.

You have probably seen paintings showing Salome and the decapitated head on a platter. The subject has fascinated artists and writers, including Oscar Wilde. (In his famous play *Salome*, Herod is so appalled when Salome kisses the mouth of the dead John that Herod orders her killed.) The appeal of the subject is obvious: earthly power and lust and violence—versus a saintly prophet. Whose side are you on?

Sibling Deviltry

Brother-and-sister act, with a vengeance

Y ou may be familiar with the twelve tribes of Israel, descended
from the twelve sons of Jacob. Sons were important in ancient
times, and the more the better. But fertile Jacob did have at least
one daughter, connected with one of the most colorful—and unpleasant—stories in the Old Testament.

Her name was Dinah, and she was the daughter of Jacob and his
poor wife Leah. ("Poor" because Jacob didn't love her much, preferring
her younger, prettier sister Rachel, his other wife.) Of Jacob's brood of
twelve sons, two of them, Levi and Simeon, were also sons of Leah, thus
Dinah's full brothers.

Jacob's enormous family had camped out near the Canaanite city of
Shechem—ruled by a man named Shechem. The Bible is often blunt and
straightforward in its telling of a story: When Shechem saw Dinah, "he
seized her and lay with her and humbled her" (Gen. 34:2 RSV). In other
words, a randy Canaanite chieftain raped Jacob's daughter.

Dinah was the daughter of a wealthy man who also happened to
have twelve adult sons. In the days when fathers and daughters took a
great interest in preserving a girl's purity, Shechem's deed was headlong,
rash, and dangerous.

But the Bible is full of surprises. Ordinarily, men being what they are,
they don't feel any kind of emotional bond to a raped woman. Normally
they would throw her away like a dirty sock. (There is a story of this
in the Bible—see 2 Sam. 13.) But for some odd reason Shechem didn't
behave that way: "His soul was drawn to Dinah the daughter of Jacob;
he loved the maiden and spoke tenderly to her" (Gen. 34:3 RSV). He
asked his father to seal a marriage deal with Dinah's father.

46

Shechem and his father knew Dinah's brothers were at the boiling point. But they tried their best to smooth things over, asking Jacob and sons to dwell among them, intermarry with the locals, and live together in peace and prosperity. Under the circumstances, Shechem was doing the best he could. He had committed rape (bad) but claimed he loved the girl and wanted to keep her (good). We have no idea what Dinah's feelings were. The Bible doesn't say.

Dinah's brothers concocted a cunning scheme for revenge. They agreed to allow the marriage to take place—*if* Shechem and his tribesmen would let themselves be circumcised. (Remember that the Hebrews took circumcision seriously. It was a sign of their covenant with God.) Circumcision on an adult male was, to put it mildly, a painful thing—no anesthetic, no knives made of fine surgical steel. Instead, flint knives, bleeding, screaming, and several days of serious discomfort. Yet Shechem agreed to it. And somehow he and his father persuaded the local men to submit to it.

What follows is both amusing and painful to read:

> On the third day, when [the men] were sore, two of the sons of Jacob, Simeon and Levi, Dinah's brothers, took their swords and came against the city unawares and killed all the males. They slew Hamor and his son Shechem with the sword, and took Dinah out of Shechem's house and went away. (Gen. 34:25–26 RSV)

The brothers didn't stop there—they plundered the city, making off with the livestock and anything else of value.

Their father Jacob was not pleased. He feared vengeance from the other Canaanites. But Dinah's brothers made no apology: "Should he have treated our sister like a prostitute?" (Gen. 34:31).

Is there any moral message in this sordid little tale? Oddly, there is. The Israelites were always in danger of intermarrying with the surrounding nations and taking part in their pagan religious rituals—which often involved child sacrifice and ritual prostitution. Dinah's rape is a horrible thing, even if Shechem did decide to marry her. Her brothers' act of vengeance was an overreaction (over*kill*, literally) to what happened to her, but it shows us how seriously the ancient Israelites took sexual purity. If Dinah had married Shechem, and if Jacob's family had settled among the locals, there was a danger of Shechem and his kind's corruption of Israel's religion and morals.

Dinah is an individual, but you get the feeling from reading Genesis 34 that she symbolizes all Israelite women who are not safe among the immoral men of Canaan, men like Shechem. We have to wonder about Shechem's postrape marriage proposal. Was he one of those all-too-common men who fell into blind lust, then foolishly confused it with love? We can probably assume he would not have made the most faithful husband.

Four thousand years later, women still fear male sexual predators. Some things never change.

The Ultimate Dysfunctional Family

Full-blown half-sibling problems

If you think blended families have problems today, rest assured they are nothing new. They had problems in Bible times, too, particularly since men of wealth often married more than one wife, creating large households with children by different wives, and the inevitable jealousy and back-stabbing.

Israel's famous King David had numerous wives and numerous children, and inevitably one of his sons fell in lust with a half-sister. This particular son was named Amnon, and he lusted heartily after his lovely virgin half-sister Tamar. Amnon was, the Bible says, "frustrated to the point of illness on account of his sister Tamar, for she was a virgin, and it seemed impossible for him to do anything to her" (2 Sam. 13:2).

A crafty friend of Amnon suggested that he use the old sympathy ploy: play sick and arrange for Tamar to comfort him. Tamar baked him some bread as he requested, but when she brought it to him, he uttered some of the most disgusting words in the whole Bible: "Come to bed with me, my sister" (2 Sam. 13:11).

Naturally Amnon had made sure no one else was present when this happened. Tamar was horrified, and as she would not give in willingly, Amnon raped her.

The story would be horrible enough if it had ended there, but things got worse: "Then Amnon hated her with intense hatred. In fact, he hated her more than he had loved her. Amnon said to her, 'Get up and get out!'" (2 Sam. 13:15). Amnon called his personal servant and had Tamar thrown out bodily, and he bolted the door behind her.

So, Amnon the king's son had raped Tamar the king's daughter—not only raped her, but callously threw her out afterward. To show her grief, Tamar put ashes on her head and tore her royal robe, the usual signs of mourning and sadness in the ancient world.

Tamar had a loyal brother—her *full* brother, that is—named Absalom. Tamar went to live in Absalom's house, and Absalom proved he could exercise great self-control, for he said not a word good or bad about what had happened to Tamar. Apparently Absalom believed the old proverb that "revenge is best when served up cold." A full two years after the rape of Tamar, Absalom had his servants murder Amnon. Appropriately, the roguish Amnon was drunk at the time. Absalom fled and lived in exile for three years.

Though David mourned the loss of Amnon, he apparently was more concerned over his other son: "The spirit of the king longed to go to Absalom" (2 Sam. 13:39).

Under the circumstances, it is hard to fault Absalom for his violent act. Amnon had done something truly detestable, not only raping Tamar but treating her shamefully afterward. David had proven himself to be an inadequate father, making no attempt to punish Amnon in any way, so Absalom took matters into his own hands. David was a passionate man, married to many wives, and apparently Absalom inherited his nature. Too bad David wasn't passionate enough about justice and discipline to keep his numerous progeny in line.

Whatever became of poor Tamar? We don't know. In ancient times, a raped woman was damaged goods, so it is unlikely she ever married. Her loyal brother Absalom thought well enough of her that he named one of his own daughters Tamar. The Bible mentions that this younger Tamar "became a beautiful woman" (2 Sam. 14:27).

Worth noting: Amnon and Absalom were the king's oldest sons. Had Amnon lived, he would have been the logical successor as king of Israel. Obviously it was no loss to Israel that this immoral man never reigned as king. With Amnon dead, Absalom became the heir apparent. It is probably safe to assume that he murdered Amnon not only because of his concern for Tamar, but also because of his own desire for the throne of Israel. Amnon's despicable act had provided Absalom with a wonderful excuse to get Amnon out of the way.

Absalom, like Amnon, never did become king. And he was to cause much more trouble for his father further down the line.

Any lessons to be learned from this sordid story? One logical one is, don't father children by several wives. While polygamy is not legal, serial polygamy (marrying, divorcing, remarrying, divorcing, etc.) is legal, and many blended families today experience problems just as dramatic as those of David's household.

Another lesson: parents ought to take a firmer hand than David did. We are told that after learning of the rape of Tamar, David "was furious" (2 Sam. 13:21)—yet he did nothing about the situation. We can assume his wrath subsided quickly, and he shrugged the matter off—"Boys will be boys, so just let the matter drop." Clearly that was not the wisest, or fairest, way to deal with this matter, and thanks to the king's negligence, Amnon ended up dead, and Absalom began nurturing a power hunger that would result in further disasters for himself and David, too. David could have taken some lessons in tough love.

Saul the Heretic

—◆—

Was blind, but now I see

If you love art museums, you have no doubt seen paintings with such titles as *The Conversion of Paul*. The dramatic, life-changing conversion has fascinated artists throughout the centuries, and rightly so. The scene is spiritually interesting because the great persecutor of Christians changed into one of the great Christian missionaries. And it is visually interesting because artists must draw on their craft and creativity to try to show the divine light that blinded the persecutor.

The first mention of Saul occurs in Acts 8:1. He was present when the Jews stoned to death the great Christian speaker Stephen, who became the first martyr for the faith. "And Saul was there, giving approval to his death." And no wonder. This young man Saul was a true zealot, an intense man who loved God and the Jewish religion passionately, a man who wanted no compromise with the philosophies and religions of the non-Jewish world. He saw Stephen and the Christians as heretics, a threat to the purity of Judaism. They had to be silenced—either through persuasion or failing that, through violence. Stephen had been a heretic and a blasphemer, in Paul's eyes, and the Jews of Jerusalem had been right to destroy him.

When we meet with Saul again in Acts 9:1, he was "still breathing out murderous threats against the Lord's disciples." He got the official approval of the high priest in Jerusalem to journey to the city of Damascus to seek out any Jews there who might have converted to "the Way," as Acts sometimes calls Christianity. His intention was to take these heretics back to Jerusalem as prisoners. His plans got changed in a dramatic way, and before long he would find himself being taken prisoner.

> As he neared Damascus on his journey, suddenly a light from heaven flashed around him. He fell to the ground and heard a voice say to him, "Saul, Saul, why do you persecute me?"
>
> "Who are you, Lord?" Saul asked.
>
> "I am Jesus, whom you are persecuting." (Acts 9:3–5)

In a few short sentences, Luke sums up one of the most dramatic, world-changing encounters of all time.

We can assume that Luke, the author of Acts, had this account from Saul (later Paul) himself. But apparently the heavenly voice was audible to others, for Saul's companions were astounded, struck speechless— and Saul himself was sightless. "So they led him by the hand into Damascus. For three days he was blind, and did not eat or drink anything" (Acts 9:8–9).

Saul did not remain blind. A Christian named Ananias healed him. Ananias had received his own message from God, one that frightened him: God told him to go meet with the malicious persecutor Saul. Ananias protested, but God assured him that Saul would be the "chosen instrument to carry my name before the Gentiles and their kings and before the people of Israel" (Acts 9:15).

Ananias did as he was instructed. Placing his hands on Saul, he said, "Brother Saul, the Lord—Jesus who appeared to you on the road as you were coming here—has sent me so that you may see again and be filled with the Holy Spirit." As Luke puts it, "something like scales fell from Saul's eyes, and he could see again" (Acts 9:17–18). The former persecutor was then baptized—and then took some food. Apparently the spiritual had priority over the physical.

Ananias was not the only Christian who was at first skeptical of Saul. Others were suspicious of this man who had traveled to Damascus initially to persecute them. Was he really a new Christian, or was this some kind of trick? But Paul won them over with his zeal and sincerity. All the intensity he had put to use in persecuting the faith he now put to use in spreading that faith.

And now, naturally, his former allies the Jews despised him. The former defender of their faith had become (horrors!) a Christian—in their eyes, a blasphemer and heretic. In an ironic twist, Saul had gone to Damascus to persecute Christians on behalf of the Jews—and had to leave the city for fear of the Jews. They plotted to kill him, and the plot involved keeping watch over the city's gates. The Christians' solution: instead of having him exit through a gate, they lowered him in a basket over the city walls. Not a dignified exit, certainly, but it preserved the life of the man who did more than anyone else to spread the faith in its early years.

Much of the rest of the book of Acts is a kind of an appendix to this dramatic story: Saul the zealous Jew believed Christianity was the fulfillment of the Jews' hopes, so he spread the Christian message wherever he went, converting some Jews and angering many others. Most of his various adventures and trials were due to his raising the ire of his fellow Jews. But Saul (more later about his name change to Paul) knew he was not a heretic or blasphemer. Like all faithful Jews, he had awaited God's Messiah. He firmly believed that Jesus was the Messiah, so he followed him.

Saul's story has been repeated endlessly throughout history; a person who commits himself fully to the faith inevitably makes enemies of his former associates. They view him as a traitor or a heretic, and while they may not go so far as to try to kill him, they may persecute him or ostracize him. But people of faith will always do as Saul did: cling to their faith, assured that they really did encounter Christ.

Incidentally, Christians have traditionally taken Saul's conversion so seriously that the Catholic and Anglican churches celebrate it every January 25.

Mountain of Metamorphosis

Jesus and some glorious company

You may have occasionally seen a church with the name *Church of the Transfiguration*. Have any idea what that means? "Transfiguration" is one way of translating the Greek word *metamorphosis*, which literally means "change of shape" or "change of form." The three synoptic Gospels (Matthew, Mark, and Luke, that is) all refer to a mysterious, awe-inspiring incident in the life of Jesus, an incident that Christian tradition calls the Transfiguration.

You'll find the story in Matthew 17:1–8, Mark 9:2–8, and Luke 9:28–36. In all three accounts, Jesus took his inner circle of disciples—Peter, James, and John—to a high mountain. There before them he was "transfigured": his clothing became dazzling white, "whiter than anyone in the world could bleach them" (Mark 9:3). And with him appeared two notable figures from Israel's past, Moses and Elijah, both conversing with the beaming Jesus.

You don't have to be all that familiar with the Bible to know that Moses is one of its major characters. He was the great liberator, who confronted the oppressive Egyptian pharaoh and then led his people from slavery in Egypt to their homeland in Canaan. It was through Moses that God delivered the Law, the divine code of moral and ritual rules. In the Jews' tradition, Moses was not only an honored individual but also a symbol of the Law itself.

Elijah was likewise an important character, the great wilderness prophet who boldly confronted the wicked King Ahab and his equally wicked wife, Jezebel. More important, Elijah held out for the worship of the true God when so many people in Israel were bowing down to idols.

As Moses represented the sacred tradition of the Law, so Elijah represented the prophets.

Impressive as these two men were, their deaths were mysterious. Elijah did not die at all but was taken into heaven in a chariot drawn by fiery horses. Moses did die, but Deuteronomy says that God himself buried Moses, and no human being knows where his grave is (see Deut. 34:5). A later Jewish tradition says that the great Moses himself did not die, but was, like Elijah, taken into heaven.

Now, back to the Transfiguration: The Gospels tell us that Jesus, Moses, and Elijah were conversing on the mountain. Luke's Gospel notes that they were talking "about his departure, which he was about to bring to fulfillment at Jerusalem" (Luke 9:31)—that is, the three were talking about Jesus' forthcoming crucifixion. Clearly these two heavenly figures took a great interest in that event.

As if the scene weren't already dramatic enough, "a cloud appeared and enveloped them . . . A voice came from the cloud, saying, 'This is my Son, whom I have chosen; listen to him'" (Luke 9:34–35). If those words sound familiar, they are very similar to the words of approval that God spoke at Jesus' baptism.

The disciples were, needless to say, awestruck at the event. They had seen their Master perform numerous miracles, but this was the first time they had seen him appear in a state of glory. Matthew's Gospel says that the three disciples fell facedown on the ground. When they looked up, the cloud, the radiance, and Moses and Elijah were all gone.

The Gospels add an amusing detail to the story: the loyal (and often rash) Peter made the suggestion that the disciples could set up three shelters—one each for Jesus, Moses, and Elijah. Meaning what, exactly? Apparently Peter was so impressed by the dazzling event that he wanted to set up a sort of shrine to commemorate it. Mark's Gospel notes that "he did not know what to say, they were so frightened" (9:6). And who wouldn't have been?

Christian tradition has read a lot of significance into the story. As at Jesus' baptism, God gave Jesus a word of approval. Jesus appeared with two of the greatest men in Jewish tradition, which tells us he was worthy to be in the company of Israel's spiritual giants. And his divinity was, momentarily, unveiled for his disciples to see.

Walking with him every day through Galilee and Judea, the disciples saw a Jewish carpenter, an ordinary human being who was an extraordinary teacher and at times, a miracle worker. But on the mountain the three disciples saw his true colors—the Son of God himself. Peter, in one of his two letters found in the New Testament, referred to the event, reminding his readers that he himself was an eyewitness to Jesus' majesty (2 Pet. 1:16–18).

The Catholic, Eastern Orthodox, and Anglican churches celebrate the Feast of the Transfiguration every August 6. Tourists in the Holy Land can still get a glimpse at the mountain where the event took place—on either Mount Hermon or Mount Tabor.

Does the event have any take-home value for readers today? Of course it does. It is a reminder to Christians to take their "everyday Jesus" a little more seriously. We tend to think of Jesus as a nice man who went about doing good and who said many things that make very nice quotations. He was all that—but, as the Transfiguration makes clear, much more than that also. He was a truly glorious (in the full sense) person. And as the apostles would learn after his crucifixion and resurrection, an even more significant figure than either the great Moses or Elijah was.

The Original Camel Jockeys

Animal jewelry for pirates of the land

The world's original "camel jockeys" were the Midianites, who were skilled riders and feared raiders. These nomadic people occupied the area east of the Jordan River, as well as part of the Sinai Peninsula, that big wedge of land connecting Asia and Africa. It was Midianite trader-raiders who sold Joseph, Jacob's son, into slavery in Egypt (Gen. 37). When Moses fled from Egypt, he lived in Midian, and there he married a daughter of the Midianite priest Jethro (Exod. 2).

Ironically, though, years later when the Israelites left Egypt and journeyed toward Canaan, God commanded Moses and the Israelites to kill all the Midianites, who were their enemies (Num. 25:16–18). Long after this, the military leader Gideon had to free Israel from the oppression of the Midianites, who were "like swarms of locusts" that "did not spare a living thing" (Judg. 6:5, 4). The Midianites allowed Israelites to plow and sow their seed, but the Midianites destroyed the crops.

The story of Gideon's defeat of a much larger Midianite force is well told in Judges 7. Gideon and his three hundred men staged a clever ruse, blowing trumpets and breaking jars, creating such a ruckus that the Midianites thought they were facing an enormous army. The battle cry of the Israelites is memorable: "A sword for the LORD and for Gideon!" (Judg. 7:20).

The Midianites and Israelites were, in fact, very distant cousins. The Israelites traced their ancestry back to the patriarch Abraham, and through Abraham's son Isaac. The Midianites were also descendants of Abraham, but through Midian, Abraham's son by his concubine. As you might have gathered from the previous paragraph, this family connection did not endear the Midianites and Israelites to each other. Though

Moses had married a Midianite woman, and though his father-in-law acknowledged Israel's God as supreme, the father-in-law could not bring himself to join Israel (Exod. 18).

Some nations took great pride in their fierceness, and certainly the Midianites did. You can see this in the name of their chieftains: *Zebah*, which means "a slaying"; *Oreb*, which means "raven" (a bird connected with dead bodies); and *Zeeb*, which means "wolf."

Apparently all this fierceness paid off. The book of Numbers reports that in the time of Moses they had 675,000 sheep, 72,000 oxen, and 61,000 donkeys (Num. 31:32–34). Also, "their camels could no more be counted than the sand on the seashore" (Judg. 7:12). (If you read the Old Testament, you learn quickly that wealth was not measured in terms of money or acres of land, but in livestock.) They also possessed great stores of gold, silver, brass, iron, tin, and lead.

And that brings us to the reason we include the Midianites in this book: they were so fond of their camels, which they used effectively in their military raids, that they dressed their camels well—specifically, their camels wore gold chains around their necks (Judg. 8:26). Clearly a people who could deck their beasts of burden in gold jewelry were living well.

But then, as the Bible doesn't fail to point out, their gold and other possessions were all ill-gotten gains, wealth they gained by robbing and oppressing others. The Bible lumps the Midianites with other "people of the East" (Judg. 6:3 RSV), people who lived as land pirates and were feared and despised by the many other tribes they oppressed. When Gideon and his men defeated the Midianites in battle, the camel necklaces were among the loot they took.

Happily, Gideon's defeat of the Midianites marked the end of their harassing of Israel. Later generations remembered fondly this defeat as "the day of Midian" (Isa. 9:4 RSV). The Bible occasionally mentions them as traders in gold and incense, but their days as raiders in the territory of Israel were gone. Certainly the Israelites did not miss them much.

In one sense, the Bible is painful to read, for in it we see that God's people were always being oppressed by wicked people. So we need to remind ourselves oppressive peoples such as the Midianites have their day and disappear from the pages of history, while faith in the true God endures.

Peter's Rooftop Buffet

A tarp with unclean critters

Have you ever noticed the connection between religion and food? In today's most popular religion (the cult of self-worship, that is), people are supposed to avoid fat, cholesterol, red meat, sugar, etc. In the Jewish religion, people avoid "unclean" foods—that is, nonkosher items, according to the laws found in Leviticus 11. Pork is forbidden, and so are shellfish and rabbit. Most of the "unclean" creatures are ones the majority of us would avoid anyway: most insects, vultures, ravens, gulls, owls, storks, bats, rats, weasels, lizards, and so on.

What about Christianity? Strictly speaking, Christianity has no food laws. Even though Jesus and his first followers were Jews, Christians rather quickly abandoned the dietary laws. Mark 7 records Jesus' confrontations with the Pharisees, who criticized him for not being fastidious about the Jewish food laws. Jesus told his listeners that "nothing outside a man can make him 'unclean' by going into him. Rather, it is what comes out of a man that makes him 'unclean'" (v. 15)—that is, unclean words or actions. Jesus, in saying this, declared that all foods were "clean."

Even so, there is no evidence that the first Jewish Christians changed their dietary patterns. Old habits die hard: a faithful Jew was not going to start eating pork just because he had become a Christian. But what about pagans who converted to Christianity? It must have pleased them to learn that though Christianity had a strict morality, it did not have strict (and pointless) rules about diet. The moral laws of the Jewish religion were not done away with, but the ritual laws were.

We see this in Acts 10, where we meet an appealing character named Cornelius, a Roman centurion. The author of Acts describes him as "devout and God-fearing" (v. 2), which meant he practiced a Jewish spirituality, including prayer and aiding the poor. The Bible also mentions that an angel visited him and linked him up with the apostle Peter.

Praying on the rooftop of a house, Peter had a curious vision: a large sheet (or *tarp* might be more accurate) was let down from heaven. In it were all kinds of animals, including reptiles. Peter was hungry at the time, and a voice said, "Get up, Peter. Kill and eat." Apparently all the creatures in the tarp were nonkosher, for Peter protested, "I have never eaten anything impure or unclean." The heavenly voice spoke again: "Do not call anything impure that God has made clean" (Acts 10:13–15). This happened three times, and the tarp was taken back to heaven.

Peter puzzled over what this all meant. While he was still puzzling, messengers from Cornelius found him.

Peter's vision was a turning point in Christianity: God was telling him to take the Christian faith to non-Jews. "I now realize how true it is that God does not show favoritism but accepts men from every nation who fear him and do what is right" (Acts 10:34–35). He met with Cornelius, even though Jewish custom required him to avoid the homes of non-Jews. Cornelius's whole household converted to Christianity.

Peter's fellow Christians called him on the carpet for hobnobbing with non-Jews, but Peter explained his vision, and the other Christians rejoiced that God had included non-Jews in his plan of salvation. "God has granted even the Gentiles repentance unto life" (Acts 11:18). The faith wasn't going to be just a splinter group of Judaism: it would be a universal faith for people everywhere.

Each one of us needs to keep Peter's vision in mind. We no longer share Peter's former prejudices about Jews and Gentiles, of course, but each of us has some prejudices about what type of people God wants to save. The Bible makes it clear enough: *all* types. But we are all inclined to favor our own group, "our kind of people," people who share our own skin color or income level or education level. We forget that God desires that the gospel be spread to everyone, even the people that may be "unclean" in our view of the world.

The Big Wedding Night Switcheroo

The ultimate bad in-law story

I f you like romance, or stories about romance, you won't find much of it in the Bible. There is the Song of Solomon, of course, but elsewhere the Bible pays little attention to male-female attraction. It isn't opposed to romance—and certainly not opposed to lasting love. But for the Bible writers, romance was definitely a low priority.

The scarcity of romance makes the story of Jacob and Rachel that much more distinctive. Jacob, you might recall, was the grandson of the patriarch Abraham, and Jacob became the father of the twelve sons whose offspring became the twelve tribes of Israel. But our present concern is the childless Jacob, the bachelor who fell deeply in love with his pretty cousin, Rachel.

Her father, Laban, was Jacob's uncle, and Laban showed kindness to his nephew—for a while, anyway. Then Laban proved himself to be the most crafty and unscrupulous uncle (and father-in-law) imaginable.

Laban knew Jacob was smitten with Rachel, so he made a proposal: Jacob would work for him seven years, and after that he could marry Rachel. Jacob agreed, which tells you something about his infatuation for the woman. "So Jacob served seven years to get Rachel, but they seemed like only a few days to him because of his love for her" (Gen. 29:20).

Sounds romantic, yes? As you might imagine, Jacob was looking forward to his wedding day—and night. Laban gave a lavish wedding party. We aren't told exactly how, but when the merry Jacob went to bed that night, it was not with Rachel, but with her less attractive older sister, Leah. We can assume that as the bride was led to the wedding chamber (or tent, to be accurate), she was veiled, and Jacob had probably had plenty of wine. At any rate, the next morning, Jacob was furious.

His deceptive uncle had the perfect excuse for what had happened: "It is not our custom here to give the younger daughter in marriage before the older one" (Gen. 29:26). You can imagine Jacob thinking, *Fine, you might have told me that earlier—say, seven years ago.* But instead of packing up in anger and heading home, Jacob labored another seven years to get Rachel—but happily for him, he got Rachel at the beginning of those seven years, not at the end.

Thanks to Laban's deceit, Jacob had two wives, one he loved and one he really did not. As you might imagine, that did not make for a happy home life. As a compensation for poor Leah not being loved, God allowed her to have children, while Rachel was having none. Rachel got so frustrated, she asked Jacob to sleep with her maid, Bilhah. Strange as it seems to us, Bilhah's children would be, in some sense, Rachel's.

In the meantime, Leah stopped having children, so she, too, offered her maid to Jacob. At long last, Rachel, the one woman Jacob really loved, did have sons. So Jacob's twelve sons were the children of Leah, Rachel, and the wives' maids. (Since Jacob was fathering children by the maids, the two would have been considered his concubines, not just servants.) Such a family.

Genesis presents Jacob as a scheming, cunning character. The story of Laban pulling his wedding night switcheroo on Jacob makes us aware that even crafty characters get used and deceived by other crafty characters.

The Seven-Day
Wonder of Israel

King Zimri and his blazing finish

In a list of the kings of Israel, you will find the name *Zimri*. He reigned a grand total of seven days, and he went out with a bang. Curious? Read on.

You may know already that the kingdom of Israel had split into two separate countries after the death of Solomon. While Solomon was noted for his wealth and wisdom (and his dozens of wives and concubines), his son Rehoboam was an arrogant brat, and ten of the twelve tribes of Israel rejected him as their king. They broke away from the other two tribes and went by the name Israel (also called the "northern kingdom"). The remaining two tribes, Judah and Benjamin, were known as the kingdom of Judah (the "southern kingdom"), with the capital still in Jerusalem.

Following the breakup of the kingdom (see 1 Kings 12), the books of 1 and 2 Kings begin an alternating pattern, giving us data on a king of Judah, then a king of Israel, then a king of Judah, and so on. As a group, the kings of both countries were a sorry lot, but there were a few saintly ones among the kings of Judah.

And oddly, while Judah had its political and social problems, its king was always a descendant of the first king, the famous David. By contrast, the Bible has hardly anything good to say about the kings of Israel. And instead of one continuous dynasty, as Judah had, Israel never had any stability in regard to its ruling families.

If you don't like violence, then don't read 1 and 2 Kings. They were violent times, and the Bible pulls no punches as it tells the sordid tales of the kings and the various plots against them. In 1 Kings 16 we learn that the king of Israel was (temporarily) a man named Elah. Baasha, Elah's father, had reigned twenty-four years. Elah would reign only two, and we soon find out why: "Zimri, one of his officials, who had command of half his chariots, plotted against him. Elah was in Tirzah at the time, getting drunk in the home of Arza, the man in charge of the palace at Tirzah. Zimri came in, struck him down and killed him . . . Then he succeeded him as king" (1 Kings 16:9–10). A lovely scene: a drunk king, murdered by one of his own officials.

Once Zimri started killing, he could not stop. Elah's family would not sit idly by after Elah's murder, so Zimri killed off every relative or friend of the family. According to 1 Kings, Elah's family was being paid back for all the evil it had done. Such is the way of justice in this world: loathsome people are sometimes eliminated by other loathsome people. The Bible has no praise for Zimri, but it does approve of the justice done to Elah's wicked family.

Now, here is a puzzle: 1 Kings tells us that Zimri slaughtered all the members of Elah's family. Then it tells us that he reigned a mere *seven days*. Wow. That was a lot of murdering for seven days. It is probably safe to assume that he had been plotting his coup for a long time, and that he had a lot of accomplices in his murder spree.

The Israelites as a whole had no intention of accepting the usurper Zimri as king, so they made Omri, commander of Israel's army, the new king. Omri took the army to the capital city, Tirzah, and captured it. Zimri was no fool: he knew that under the circumstances he wasn't going to escape with his life. So, in one of the most dramatic suicides ever, he "set the palace on fire around him" (1 Kings 16:18). He went out in a blaze, but not a blaze of glory.

Omri turned out to be a wicked king, too, but he had a more stable reign, and he passed the throne on to his very famous son, the notorious Ahab. You might recall that Ahab's wife was the idol-worshiping Jezebel, who years later lost her life in another of Israel's many military coups. A man named Jehu led this particular coup, and he was happy to rid the land of the vile Jezebel.

Facing Jehu just before he had her killed, Jezebel threw a taunt at him: "Did Zimri have peace, who murdered his master?" (2 Kings 9:31 AP). She expected Jehu to remember Zimri, the man who had seized the throne from the king—and did not live to enjoy a long reign afterward.

Her last words were priceless: in effect, she was telling Jehu, "You may kill me, little man, but don't expect any peace yourself."

Any usurper had to face the same situation as Zimri: someone else waiting to capture the throne. If you kill the king, you may seize his throne, but you won't ever be able to sleep soundly, knowing the same thing can happen to you. If you live violently, you can expect to die violently.

Red or Reed, Awesome Either Way

That famous water stunt—but not where you thought it was

B race yourself. Here are three facts:

1. God did not part the Red Sea for the Israelites.
2. The Israelites never even crossed the Red Sea.
3. The Bible does not say that they did.

You may at this moment be thumbing through your Bible to check out that third item. And it is possible that your version of the Bible may actually say the Israelites crossed the "Red Sea." But it is wrong. God did perform a truly amazing water miracle, but not at the Red Sea. Read on.

Consider for a moment what, and where, the Red Sea actually is. It is a long and skinny arm of the Indian Ocean, with the continent of Africa on its west side and Arabia on its east side. Its northern end is at the famous Sinai Peninsula, where the nations of Egypt and Jordan border each other today. There are bigger seas, but the Red Sea is quite large— more than a thousand miles long, and from 150 to 250 miles wide. At its northern end, the Sinai Peninsula splits the Red Sea into two skinnier bodies of water, the Gulf of Suez and the Gulf of Aqaba. (And in case you were curious, the sea gets its name from the reddish algae that at times tints its waters.)

Geography lesson ended (for now), and back to God and the Israelites: under Moses' leadership, the Israelites had been released from their slavery in Egypt and were headed toward their ancestral homeland, Canaan. That is, they were headed in a northeasterly direction. According to Exodus 13, "God led the people around by the desert toward the

Red Sea" (v. 18). Looking at any map of this area, you would see they would cross the sea at its far northern end, perhaps at the Gulf of Suez.

But in fact, the original Hebrew version of Exodus does not say they were at the Red Sea. The Hebrew original refers to the body of water as the *yam suph*—"Reed Sea" or "Sea of Reeds" or even "Marshy Sea." This was most definitely not the same as the Red Sea. (In fact, the Red Sea has no reeds in it. Reeds are freshwater plants, not saltwater.) A few newer translations of the Bible have "Reed Sea" instead of "Red Sea," but most stick with "Red Sea" and then mention in a footnote that *yam suph* means "Sea of Reeds."

Centuries ago, when the Hebrew Bible was translated into Greek, the Hebrew *yam suph* made it into Greek as *erythra thalassa*—"Red Sea." Centuries after that, the wonderful old King James Version had "Red Sea," and generation after generation grew up believing that God parted the Red Sea. A very minor translation error, but one that raises the question: where was this "Reed Sea," anyway?

Remember that the Israelite slaves in Egypt inhabited a section called Goshen. Not far from Goshen was a body of water that the Egyptians referred to as the "Suph," meaning "Papyrus Marsh." (Papyrus, you might recall, was the marsh plant with the stalks that were made into the world's first paper.) This body of water is today called Lake Timsah. It is not a sea in the usual sense—that is, it is freshwater, not salt. And though it is large, it is nowhere near as huge as the Red Sea. The Bible scholars are about 90 percent certain that this Lake Timsah—the "Reed Sea"—was the body of water the Israelites crossed. It is certainly more likely that they crossed it rather than the Red Sea.

Whether it was "Reed" or "Red" is not really the point. Exodus is presenting us with a miracle, one of the most dramatic ones ever seen on earth. It certainly made for one of the great movie scenes of all time, in the Hollywood classic *The Ten Commandments*. Let's set the scene again: After God sent ten plagues on Egypt, the wicked pharaoh finally agreed to free the Israelite slaves. Moses and the thousands of Israelites set out for Canaan—and then the pharaoh changed his mind. So the pharaoh

> had his chariot made ready and took his army with him. He took six
> hundred of the best chariots, along with all the other chariots of Egypt,

with officers over all of them . . . The Egyptians—all Pharaoh's horses and chariots, horsemen and troops—pursued the Israelites and overtook them. (Exod. 14:6–9)

Naturally the Israelites panicked. They were in a tight spot: water on one side, enemy troops on the other. After getting their hopes up and setting out for freedom, they faced reenslavement—or massacre. They turned on Moses angrily. Why hadn't he just let them remain in Egypt? But Moses had more faith than that. He could not believe God would abandon them at this point.

Just as in the movie, Moses raised his staff over the waters, and they parted. (This was not Moses' power, but God's, of course.) But they did not part in a matter of seconds, as in the movie. "All that night the LORD drove the sea back with a strong east wind and turned it into dry land." We don't know precisely how long it took, but the final result was the same: the people could walk through the waters, "with a wall of water on their right and on their left" (Exod. 14:21–22).

Naturally Pharaoh's charioteers planned to follow suit. But "Moses stretched out his hand over the sea, and at daybreak the sea went back to its place. The Egyptians were fleeing toward it, and the LORD swept them back into the sea . . . Not one of them survived" (Exod. 14:27–28).

Though Lake Timsah is not nearly as large as the Red Sea, it is certainly large enough to drown in. If you have ever seen a flooded river or even a flooded creek, you know the amazing power of a "wall of water." God had saved his people and destroyed their enemies at the *yam suph*—the "Reed Sea." It was probably not as wide nor as deep as what the movie showed, but it still made quite a dramatic scene, nonetheless.

It certainly stuck in the mind of Israel. If you've read the Bible much, you know that in the Old Testament the Exodus from Egypt is *the* key event, and the parting of the sea is the high point of the whole Exodus. It was the supreme miracle of the Old Testament, the ultimate proof that God was in control of things.

Did it really happen? For those who believe in miracles, naturally the answer is yes. For those who doubt, there is the "natural" explanation: the waters parted because of a strong wind—which the Bible itself says was the cause of the parting. The wind subsided, and the waters converged again. All perfectly natural—yet how was this natural occurrence timed so perfectly that the Israelites passed through while the Egyptians were drowned? Isn't it better to assume that a powerful, compassionate Someone was behind all the remarkable events?

One more thing: you now know that the Israelites crossed the Reed Sea, not the Red Sea. But if, out of long habit, you find yourself saying or thinking that "God parted the Red Sea," that's fine. The main point is that you know something truly remarkable took place. God does not grade us on geography.

Revisiting the
Tongues-of-Fire Story

———

Undoing the Tower of Babel

A hundred years ago, who would have predicted the amazing growth of Pentecostal churches? In terms of numbers, they were the great success story of the twentieth century, and they continue to grow in the twenty-first. In the U.S., Latin America, Asia, and elsewhere, Pentecostal churches grow while so many other churches decline. If you asked the Pentecostals themselves to explain this, they would give you a simple answer: "the Holy Spirit."

The Christian church never totally forgot about the Holy Spirit, of course. But for many centuries the Spirit was simply a name ministers used in the ritual of baptism ("In the name of the Father, and the Son, and the Holy Spirit"), and most Christians knew little and cared less about the role of the Spirit in the Christian life. This tells us that people were not reading their Bibles very closely, for the New Testament mentions the Spirit quite often, and the book of Acts in particular is brimming over with stories about the power of the Spirit.

One of the most dramatic of these is near the beginning of Acts. Jesus had ascended into heaven already, having promised his disciples that "you will receive power when the Holy Spirit comes on you" (1:8). The disciples returned to Jerusalem, and soon came the Jewish holy day known as Pentecost, a festival also called the "feast of weeks" and the "feast of first fruits." The Jews also celebrated it as the anniversary of God giving his divine law to Moses at Mount Sinai. In short, Pentecost was a red-letter day for the Jews, and it was common for Jerusalem to be filled with Jews from all over the world at this time.

On this particular Pentecost, Jesus' disciples were gathered together in a house, and suddenly a sound like the blowing of a violent wind came from heaven and filled the whole house . . . They saw what seemed to be tongues of fire that separated and came to rest on each of them. All of them were filled with the Holy Spirit and began to speak in other tongues as the Spirit enabled them. (Acts 2:2–4)

This, in case you didn't already know it, is why the name *Pentecostal* is associated with Christians who emphasize the power of the Spirit, especially the ability to speak in other tongues.

It is appropriate that the disciples experienced a "violent wind" at the time. In the Old Testament, the same Hebrew word is translated "wind" or "spirit." People in the ancient world (and people today, for that matter) understood wind as a powerful but invisible force, and God's Spirit was like that—unseen, but very powerful.

What about those "tongues of fire"? Fire, like wind, was also a symbol of God's presence. Think back to the book of Exodus, with God appearing to Moses in the form of the burning bush. In the Gospels, John the Baptist predicted the coming of someone who would baptize people "with the Holy Spirit and with fire" (Matt. 3:11).

So on this day of Pentecost, Jesus' disciples were experiencing divine power in a big way—a mighty wind and tongues of fire. A "tongue of fire" was resting on each disciple, a sign that God was empowering them individually. And so, quite miraculously, the Spirit enabled the disciples to speak in languages they had not learned—the various languages spoken by the many Jews gathered in Jerusalem for Pentecost.

Then, "a crowd came together in bewilderment, because each one heard them speaking in his own language. Utterly amazed, they asked, 'Are not all these men who are speaking Galileans? Then how is it that each of us hears them in his own native language?'" (Acts 2:6–8). How indeed. The account goes on to list the various provinces from which the people hailed. The upshot: somehow these Galileans who were followers of Jesus Christ were suddenly able to speak in various languages.

If you don't believe in miracles, you can simply write this story off as a lie, an attempt to impress the reader with a made-up tale about people speaking in languages they had not learned. If you don't believe, you will also brush aside stories of later Christian missionaries who, quite without explanation, could sometimes communicate in languages they did not know.

But clearly the author of Acts really did believe a genuine miracle had taken place. People from various parts of the Roman empire were hearing Galileans speak in their own tongues. How? The answer of Acts: the Holy Spirit. Somehow his power had broken down one of the basic human barriers—difference in languages. It does not happen all the time, of course, but clearly the first Christians believed it happened on that Pentecost.

Think back to Genesis, to the story of the Tower of Babel in chapter 11. "Now the whole world had one language and a common speech." People decided to build a tower that would reach "to the heavens." Obviously some serious pride was at work here, and God chose to thwart this prideful project: "Come, let us go down and confuse their language so they will not understand each other" (11:1, 4, 7). Thanks to this serious communication breakdown, the project was scuttled. This is the Bible's explanation for why human beings speak different languages.

Very early Christians observed that Pentecost was "Babel in reverse." At Babel, man's separateness due to language was a kind of curse for human pride. At Pentecost, the Spirit undoes the curse, enabling the preacher of the gospel to communicate with the foreigner.

Christians argue a lot about the subject of speaking in tongues. Acts mentions it often, but many later Christians claimed that the gift of tongues had passed away with the generation of the apostles. Today's Pentecostals and charismatics would state firmly, "No way!" for they believe Christians today can (and should) speak in tongues.

Whatever their views on that controversial subject, people of faith ought to agree that something miraculous—something quite unexplainable—happened on that first Pentecost after Jesus' ascension. The person of faith responds to the event not with "How did it happen?" but with "Isn't that wonderful?"

Reptilian Chitchat

Revisiting the oft-told Eden story, and that clever snake

Was that serpent in the garden of Eden really Satan himself? The Bible never actually says so, though Jews and Christians have for centuries assumed this was the case. The book of Genesis never mentions Satan or the devil by name, and the Old Testament barely mentions him at all. We have to wonder: did the author of Genesis think he was writing about Satan in disguise—or just a clever (and evil) reptile?

Whether he was the devil or not, the serpent was the first villain in the Bible. He was the first liar as well: he told Eve that, contrary to what God had said, man and woman had much to gain by eating the forbidden fruit. In fact, they would be like gods! Eve believed, ate the fruit, then gave some to Adam. Naturally they discovered (too late!) that the creature had lied. They had disobeyed God, and instead of living forever in the paradise of Eden, they were sent away to scratch out a living from the soil, woman cursed with the pain of childbirth, man cursed by having to live "by the sweat of his brow" (Gen. 3:19 AP).

The serpent did not go unpunished:

> The LORD God said to the serpent, "Because you have done this,
> Cursed are you above all the livestock
> and all the wild animals!
> You will crawl on your belly and you will eat dust
> all the days of your life.
> And I will put enmity between you and the woman,
> and between your offspring and hers;
> he will crush your head, and you will strike his heel." (Gen. 3:14–15)

Interesting, isn't it? Part of the curse caused the serpent to crawl on the ground—meaning that, prior to this, it may have walked upright, or lived in trees. If you've ever seen Michelangelo's famous pictures from Genesis (on the ceiling of the Vatican's Sistine Chapel), you might recall that the Eden serpent has a human torso and head, ending in a typical snakelike tail—but he is coiled around a tree trunk at the time of the temptation. In some Jewish legends, the precurse serpent was beautiful and even had legs.

Genesis fails to mention another aspect of the curse: obviously the snake could no longer talk. One of the curiosities of the Genesis story is that Eve does not appear shocked that the snake speaks. Had it spoken before? We aren't told. One thing we are told is that Adam and Eve were to have dominion over all living things. In other words, the snake, even if it could speak, was an *inferior* addressing its *superior* (a human, that is). Eve's proper response to the snake's lies should have been, "Shut up! You're just a stupid animal! Why should I believe you instead of God?"

Well, we know why she believed the snake: *she wanted to*. God had given Adam and Eve all they needed, with only one restriction: don't eat from the tree of knowledge. Typical of every one of us (which is why the story is in the Bible), she wanted that forbidden fruit, as did Adam. She thought God was keeping something good from her—an idea the snake expressed so well. In fact, you could remove the snake from the story, and it would have the same result: they broke the rule, they paid the price.

Striking Down the Number One Son

The importance of getting there first

People today have a hard time grasping the importance the ancient world gave to being the firstborn child—firstborn *son* especially. God told Moses, "Consecrate to me every firstborn male. The first offspring of every womb among the Israelites belongs to me, whether man or animal" (Exod. 13:1–2). The firstborn as an heir received a double portion of the inheritance. (A firstborn animal, on the other hand, was sacrificed!) A man rejoiced greatly over the birth of his firstborn, regarding the child as the "beginning of his strength" and "opener of the womb." Every parent wanted as many children as possible, but the first was always special. (Some of Israel's neighbor nations made the firstborn "special" in an unpleasant way: sacrificing him to the gods.)

Social scientists have a name for this distinctive treatment of the firstborn: *primogeniture*, which means (surprise!) "firstborn." Israelites were not the only ones to practice primogeniture; most of the neighboring nations did as well. In Israel, the firstborn son not only got a larger inheritance when the father passed on, but also special honor while the father still lived. The firstborn enjoyed some leadership in the family and an honored place at mealtimes.

There was a flip side to this practice: sometimes the firstborn son turned out to be a serious disappointment, in spite of being treated well from the day he was born. In fact, the Bible is full of examples of younger sons taking precedence over the firstborn. Of Jacob's twelve sons, he loved the youngest (Joseph and Benjamin) more than the eldest (Reuben). Jacob himself was the younger son (the younger of *twins*, meaning his "older" brother entered the world only moments earlier), and Genesis contains the famous story of his tricking his father into

76

giving him his brother Esau's inheritance. And the most famous case of the youngest son taking precedence over his brothers is David, the shepherd boy whom God chose to be king over Israel.

But as the saying goes, the exception proves the rule. The rule of primogeniture held firm in ancient times, and even down to our own times. Today, if a parent dies and has no will, his property is divided up equally among his children. But this is a comparatively recent practice, because for centuries the primogeniture rule meant that the eldest son received a much larger portion. The practice applied to monarchs and nobles—meaning that when the king died, the throne went to the firstborn son. Ditto for nobles—a duke might have several sons, but only the oldest would inherit the title, along with a lot more wealth and property than the other sons.

In short, primogeniture is a very old and honored custom among human beings. You have to understand that to grasp the real impact of the story told in Exodus 11. You will recall from reading Exodus that God sent numerous plagues on the land of Egypt, plagues designed to convinced the Egyptian pharaoh to release the Israelite slaves. Pharaoh proved to be supremely stubborn. Each plague made Pharaoh consider releasing the slaves, but he always changed his mind—until the last plague, which was the death of the firstborn.

The earlier plagues had been unpleasant enough: the river turning to blood, then frogs, gnats, flies, livestock sickness, boils, hail, locusts, darkness. Always the Egyptians and their property suffered, never the Israelite slaves. Somehow the message had not gotten through to Pharaoh: this God of Israel was very powerful, and if he wanted his people set free, it would be wise to do so. But Pharaoh would not give up.

Then God made a promise to Moses: the tenth plague would be the final one, for when Pharaoh witnessed the firstborn among the Egyptians dying, he would relent and let the Israelites go.

The Jews still celebrate the tenth plague in their festival of Passover. God instructed Moses to have the Israelites daub their door frames with lambs' blood:

> On that same night I will pass through Egypt and strike down every firstborn—both men and animals—and I will bring judgment on all the gods of Egypt. I am the LORD. The blood will be a sign for you

on the houses where you are; and when I see the blood, I will pass over you. No destructive plague will touch you when I strike Egypt. (Exod. 12:12–13)

And this is what happened:

At midnight the LORD struck down all the firstborn in Egypt, from the firstborn of Pharaoh, who sat on the throne, to the firstborn of the prisoner, who was in the dungeon, and the firstborn of all the livestock as well. Pharaoh and all his officials and all the Egyptians got up during the night, and there was loud wailing in Egypt, for there was not a house without someone dead. (Exod. 12:29–30)

How did this occur? Exodus doesn't tell us. We know only that God "passed over" the homes of the Israelites and struck down the firstborn among the Egyptians.

Their "loud wailing" was to be expected, for the Egyptians, like all ancient peoples, had great reverence for their firstborn. Pharaoh himself must have wailed, for his own firstborn son had died. God's message had finally gotten through to him. He did not even wait until morning to summon Moses, but did so in the middle of the night. He told Moses to go, and quickly.

The other Egyptians heartily agreed. They feared they would all die if the Israelites did not leave immediately. In fact, Exodus tells us that the Egyptians were so impressed with the power of God that they not only freed the Israelite slaves but gave them gold, silver, and clothing on their way out. "So they plundered the Egyptians" (Exod. 12:36).

A wonderful and timeless story, one both Jews and Christians remember fondly. A powerful empire (Egypt) made slaves of God's people (the Israelites), yet those slaves were freed, not through their own revolt, but by the awesome power of God himself.

If you believe in miracles, you have no trouble accepting the story of the plagues and the Exodus from Egypt. But over the years scientists and others have puzzled over Exodus, wondering if there might be a "natural" explanation for all these odd occurrences. Some of these scientists have been Christians, people who believe God guided all the events, but that God accomplished them through occurrences in the world of nature.

Several years ago, one author came up with an interesting theory that explains all the plagues, including the death of the firstborn: journalist Ian Wilson's 1985 book *Exodus: The True Story* puts forward his theory that a volcanic eruption on the island of Thera around 1450 B.C. caused all the plagues as well as the tidal wave that parted the Red Sea. What about the tenth plague, the slaughter of the firstborn? Wilson claims that the previous nine plagues proved to the Egyptians that their own gods were angry with them, so they themselves slaughtered their own firstborn as the ultimate sacrifice.

Wilson isn't denying that God himself was the ultimate force behind all these plagues. He is simply saying that what the book of Exodus records as God striking down the Egyptians' firstborn was done through the hands of the Egyptians themselves, in a desperate act to appease their own gods.

An interesting theory, isn't it? After thousands of years, it would be impossible to prove, of course, and Wilson admits this. He also admits that the Exodus account is no less miraculous even if it was a volcanic eruption that was behind the various plagues on Egypt. Whatever means God employed to bring the plagues about, they were signs of his love for his people.

Herod the Great (Killer)

Rich, powerful, and loathsome

Alas, one of the nastiest characters in the Bible is known to history as "the Great." This was Herod, who had somehow made an impression on the Roman ruler Augustus, who allowed Herod to rule as king over the Jews (though only under the watchful eye of Rome). Herod knew the Jews despised him, so he tried to impress them with his many lavish building projects. His most important one was rebuilding the temple in Jerusalem, making it much more impressive than the original one built by Solomon. (The famous Wailing Wall in Jerusalem is the only part of Herod's temple still remaining.)

The project took forty-three years, and everyone who saw the renovated temple agreed it was awesome. While Herod did this to please the Jews, he was wise enough to keep the Romans happy as well, so he built the city of Caesarea (named, as you might guess, for Caesar).

Herod the Great appears only briefly in the Bible, notoriously in connection with the birth of Jesus. When Jesus was born in the town of Bethlehem, the "wise men" came from eastern lands and asked Herod where to find "the king of the Jews" (Matt. 2:2). The paranoid, egotistical Herod considered himself the only king of the Jews, and he wasn't exactly pleased to hear that he had some kind of rival, even if that rival was a newborn baby. His aides told him the Messiah would be born in Bethlehem. Herod told the wise men to find the child in Bethlehem and report back to him.

Herod also told them that he wanted to pay his own respects—which was a lie, of course. The wise men found Jesus, presented their famous gifts of gold, frankincense, and myrrh—but did not report back to Herod, having been warned in a dream to avoid doing this.

When Herod realized the wise men had failed to report back to him, he was furious. His plan to use them as tools to locate the infant Messiah had failed. So he issued a horrible edict: kill all the boys two years old or younger in the vicinity of Bethlehem. But Jesus was not among those killed. A dream warned Joseph to flee with Mary and the baby Jesus. Herod died not long after, and another dream told Joseph it was safe to return home.

Alert Bible readers have observed that Herod's act was similar to the act of Pharaoh in the book of Exodus. In both cases a cruel king ordered the mass slaughter of infants, and in both cases God made sure that his chosen one (Moses in Exodus, Jesus in the New Testament) survived the slaughter. Some skeptics have claimed that the story of Herod and the slaughter of the Bethlehem infants is pure fiction, a story Matthew added to his Gospel so that readers would say, "Ah, very impressive— Jesus is an important figure like Moses."

But the truth is that the loathsome King Herod was perfectly capable of doing what Matthew's Gospel says he did. While he was a wily politician, Herod was pathologically jealous and insecure, and he could be inhumanly cruel at times. He had the sons, brother, and mother of his second wife killed. As he aged he suffered from arteriosclerosis (hardening of the arteries, that is), and this seemed to worsen his mental state. He had his own firstborn son killed. He had lost the favor of Augustus Caesar, and this seemed to unhinge his mind even more.

So, given all that we know from historians about the man, it is not at all unlikely that he could have ordered the wholesale killing of infants in the town of Bethlehem, since he feared that this "king of the Jews" the wise men sought might really be a threat to his own political future.

Beautiful as the traditional Christmas story is, it does have the shadow of Herod hanging over it. Jesus escaped the slaughter at Bethlehem, but many infants did not. Roman Catholics, Anglicans, and some other Christians still observe December 28 as the Feast of the Holy Innocents, the innocents being the children Herod's order slaughtered. Three days after the joyous celebration of Jesus' birth, the Feast of the Holy Innocents is a reminder that in this fallen world, the innocent often suffer because of the blind cruelty of wicked and powerful people like Herod "the Great."

Saul, Paul, Paulus, Etc.

Meeting a devilish sorcerer

The book of Acts refers to the great apostle Paul as Saul, at least up until 13:13, where suddenly it calls him Paul, and he remains Paul for the rest of the New Testament. Why the change? No one is sure. His Jewish parents no doubt named him Saul (the name of the first king of Israel, you may recall), while Paul may have been his Roman name. By a funny coincidence, the name change in Acts occurs at a point where Saul had encountered a Roman official named Sergius Paulus. Some readers wonder if this official had anything to do with Saul's name change, and the Bible scholars tell us, "Probably not." We can be thankful that the apostle is known in Christian tradition as Paul, since that avoids confusion with the Saul of the Old Testament.

Acts 13 starts out at the city of Antioch, where Saul and several other Christians were notable teachers. God directed that Saul and Barnabas be "set apart" for work as missionaries. The pair, "sent on their way by the Holy Spirit," went to the Mediterranean island of Cyprus, which happened to be Barnabas's home (Acts 13:2, 4). (A little tidbit: in Greek mythology, the island was supposed to be the birthplace of Aphrodite, the goddess of love.)

Saul and Barnabas were both Jews, and they followed the usual missionary pattern of visiting the Jewish synagogues and trying to persuade the Jews there that Jesus Christ was the long-awaited Jewish Messiah. Acts mentioned that a certain John was their assistant. This was not (so the Bible scholars say) the apostle John, but the young man John Mark, Barnabas's cousin, and later on, the author of the Gospel that bears the name Mark.

The missionaries came to the city of Paphos, where the local official (he had the title "proconsul") was Sergius Paulus, "an intelligent man" who sent for them so he could hear the word of God (Acts 13:7). They had a willing convert, and a highly placed one to boot. But standing in their way was one of Sergius Paulus's aides, a sorcerer and false prophet named Bar-Jesus.

The Greek word we translate as "sorcerer" was *magos*—the same word that referred to the wise men who visited the baby Jesus. But not every *magos* was a "wise man." Some were mere magicians, perhaps dabblers in the occult, usually just outright fakes who managed to fool people enough to obtain money and influence. Acts 13 says this particular sorcerer was Jewish—meaning a renegade Jew, for the Jews did not condone sorcery and magic. Acts also refers to this Bar-Jesus as *Elymas*, which probably has the meaning "sorcerer."

This Bar-Jesus may have been a phony magician, but he was no fool. He was wise enough to see that if Sergius Paulus, his master, converted to Christianity, he would no longer require the services of a so-called sorcerer. Here is a phenomenon you see again and again through two thousand years of Christian history: dabblers in the occult fear and despise Christians. They do so with good reason; true believers have no place in their lives for sorcery and the occult.

So naturally the sorcerer opposed Saul and Barnabas. "Then Saul, who was also called Paul, filled with the Holy Spirit, looked straight at Elymas and said, 'You are a child of the devil and an enemy of everything that is right!'" (Acts 13:9–10). Saul (now Paul) did more than scold the wicked man: he pronounced a dramatic (but temporary) punishment—for a time he would be blind.

"Immediately mist and darkness came over him, and he groped about, seeking someone to lead him by the hand. When the proconsul saw what had happened, he believed, for he was amazed at the teaching about the Lord" (Acts 13:11–12). Clearly he was also amazed at the miracle. This happens several time in Acts: the apostles' teaching about Christ impresses people, but displays of miraculous power back up the teaching.

What became of the blinded sorcerer? We don't know. Acts says Paul had stated he would be blind only "for a time" (13:11) and we have no idea how long that time was. It is interesting that Paul referred to the man as "a child of the devil," for the name *Bar-Jesus* actually means "son of Jesus." Paul was making a play on the name—by opposing the work of Christian missionaries, Bar-Jesus was behaving like the son of the devil, not the son of Jesus. Paul used the term *devil*—the Greek word *diabolos*, which means "slanderer." Bar-Jesus literally was a slanderer, trying to defame the Christian missionaries so that Sergius Paulus would not convert to the faith.

Remember that Saul himself, on the road to Damascus, was struck down and temporarily blinded. From his blindness he emerged as a Christian believer. When he placed a temporary curse of blindness on Bar-Jesus, was he hoping the same thing might happen? That the opponent of the faith might be changed into a man of faith himself? We don't know if this happened, though it is pleasant to think that the wicked man might, in his state of blindness, have come to see the light. Whatever effect the miracle had on Bar-Jesus, it certainly affected Sergius Paulus for the better.

Saul's confrontation with the sorcerer reminds us of a neglected truth: sometimes it is necessary to be harsh with the truth. While the "soft answer" is best in most of life's situations, and tenderness and "friendly persuasion" are useful, sometimes Christians have to be brutal when confronting evil. Saul, "also called Paul," was proving he could be brazen and bold in spreading the gospel, and many preachers throughout the centuries have followed in his footsteps.

Pinned to the Mat by God

The universal champion wrestler versus Jacob

Regarding professional wrestling, a few people still ask, "Real or fake?" A Hebrew man named Jacob got involved in an all-night wrestling bout, and he knew it was real, for he had wrestled with God himself.

Jacob, you may recall, had a long-standing feud with his twin brother, Esau. As I've mentioned, Jacob, quite the crafty character, managed to finagle Esau out of his birthright (that is, his privileges as first-born son). Genesis 32 tells the story of Jacob preparing to meet Esau after many years, and he was not exactly looking forward to the reunion. Alone in the wilderness, Jacob encountered a mysterious "man," who wrestled with Jacob all night. Jacob didn't give up or give in easily, but the stranger managed to throw Jacob's hip out of joint.

Still, Jacob didn't let go of his opponent. In fact, he uttered the famous words, "I will not let you go until you bless me." The stranger's odd reply was, "What is your name?" Jacob answered, "Jacob," and the stranger bestowed a new name on him: "Israel, because you have struggled with God and with men and have overcome" (Gen. 32:26–28). Chances are your Bible has a footnote stating that *Israel* means "struggles with God."

The stranger, however, would not tell Jacob his own name, though he did bestow the blessing Jacob had asked for. Suddenly it was no longer a mystery to Jacob who this wrestler was: Jacob knew he had seen "God face to face, and yet my life was spared" (Gen. 32:30). He had a limp because of his hip being thrown out, yet he felt better for having met God. The limp was also a reminder that he had really wrestled, not just dreamed the whole episode.

Artists have enjoyed this story, and many museums have paintings with titles like *Jacob Wrestling with the Angel*. Sometimes the painters have shown the mysterious visitor with wings—which isn't quite right, since the Genesis account describes him as a man in form. He must have appeared quite human, yet somehow Jacob realized this was no ordinary flesh-and-blood opponent. He had seen God, which is why he named the site *Peniel*, meaning "face of God."

The episode is an interruption in the story of Jacob preparing to meet with Esau, but you can see that God's timing was perfect. Jacob was fretting over meeting Esau, yet after he wrestled with God himself, what fear did he have of mortal man? The moral of the story is so extremely clear we hardly need to state it: we need not fear human foes in our lives, not if we "wrestle with God" and survive. Most of us never meet God in physical form as Jacob did, yet we struggle in another way, facing down temptations, seeking God's blessing in a fallen world. Each person of faith is an "Israel."

The Small Poultry and "What Is It?" Diet

Quail and that mysterious "What is it?" stuff

Kids like to joke about school cafeterias, claiming those places serve a lot of "What is it?" By a funny coincidence, the ancient Israelites also had a diet of "What is it?" Read on.

Ingratitude is a common sin of human beings. You see this clearly in the book of Exodus. God had delivered the Israelite slaves from bondage in Egypt by sending various plagues on the Egyptians. Finally the Egyptian pharaoh freed the slaves. And as a dramatic finish to their time in Egypt, the Israelites had witnessed the parting of the Red Sea and the drowning of the Egyptian troops that had come to destroy them.

You would think this horde of slaves would be extremely grateful to this awesome and compassionate God. If they were, their gratitude was short-lived. They soon found themselves making a long trek through the wilderness, and for many of them the journey included intense gripe sessions.

> In the desert the whole community grumbled against Moses and Aaron. The Israelites said to them, "If only we had died by the LORD's hand in Egypt! There we sat around pots of meat and ate all the food we wanted, but you have brought us out into this desert to starve this entire assembly to death." (Exod. 16:2–3)

In other words, "We would rather be slaves again than a free people on their way to building their own nation."

Were things all that good in Egypt? Of course not. No one wants to live as a slave. But it is human nature to romanticize the past, even the very recent past, and the Israelites, facing the new (and dull) scenery of the desert, may have recalled their slave days as more pleasant than they really were.

What about the food? Their complaining would have you believe they ate like kings in Egypt. They probably didn't, although archaeologists have dug up inscriptions that tell us that laborers in ancient Egypt were reasonably well fed. Even so, weren't they still being awfully ungrateful to God, and to their leader Moses?

God was often displeased at the Israelites' grumbling, but on this occasion he did not respond with disapproval but with a simple granting of their request. And why not? His people were hungry, and they were in a wilderness region with few resources. They were probably near panic over the possibility of starving. So he sent them the world's most famous miracle food, manna.

"Then the LORD said to Moses, 'I will rain down bread from heaven for you. The people are to go out each day and gather enough for that day.'" This "bread from heaven" was "white like coriander seed and tasted like wafers made with honey" (Exod. 16:4, 31). The Israelites at first puzzled over it, so they gave it the name *manna*, meaning "What is it?" They found it on the ground every morning, and each day they collected enough of it to get them through the day.

The Bedouin people who still roam through the Middle East are familiar with a substance they call *mann*. It is the secretion of two scale insects, which live on the branches of the tamarisk, a common shrub of the desert. And it can be found in the exact region the Israelites were passing through.

Was this the same as the manna spoken of in Exodus 16? We aren't sure. Manna and the Bedouins' *mann* are similar, but not quite the same. Like the miraculous manna, the *mann* does not melt as the temperature rises, and it does not breed maggots (Exod. 16:20–21). Aside from that, the God-sent manna could miraculously adapt itself to the individual's needs and to the Sabbath (Exod. 16:17–18, 22–27). Also, *mann* is strictly a seasonal phenomenon, lasting only for a few weeks during summer. If the manna was the same as the naturally occurring *mann* of the region, it is clear that God somehow altered it to fit the special needs of the Israelites at that time.

Whatever manna was, it must have been nutritious enough to survive on, for it became the chief food during the Israelites' forty-year journey to Canaan. (Note Joshua 5:12: "The manna stopped the day after they ate this food from the land; there was no longer any manna for the Israelites, but that year they ate of the produce of Canaan.") Moses told Aaron, his brother and the priest of Israel, to keep a container of it as a reminder to future generations of God's care for his people (Exod. 16:33–34).

Israel never did forget manna, for they mentioned it several times in the Bible. (Consider Psalm 78:24: "He rained down manna for the people to eat, / he gave them the grain of heaven." And John 6:31: "Our forefathers ate the manna in the desert; as it is written: 'He gave them bread from heaven to eat.'") It is very likely Jesus had manna in mind when he included the words "Give us this day our daily bread" in the Lord's Prayer (Matt. 6:11 RSV). When Jesus declared that he was "the bread of life" (John 6:35), he was telling his listeners that the miraculous manna gave only physical sustenance, while he himself gave eternal life.

The other food that God miraculously provided in the wilderness was not quite so mysterious. "The LORD said to Moses, 'I have heard the grumbling of the Israelites. Tell them, "At twilight you will eat meat, and in the morning you will be filled with bread. Then you will know that I am the LORD your God.'" That evening quail came and covered the camp" (Exod. 16:11–13).

The manna was a mysterious "bread from heaven." The quails were—well, just quails. For people lacking meat, this small poultry must have been delicious.

Skeptics like to explain away the miracles of the Bible, but sometimes an obvious question remains: if something "just happened" or is just "natural," how do we account for its happening *at a particular moment in time?* Couldn't the timing be part of God's miracle as well?

Take, for example, the miraculous provision of quail for the Israelites to eat in the wilderness after they left Egypt. Many people in the past have witnessed the same amazing event described in the Old Testament: huge flocks of quail, fatigued from their long migrations over open water, land in certain areas and are so exhausted people can catch them with nets or even by hand. The Sinai Peninsula is on the quails' annual migration path, and they land there for a much-needed rest. A natural event? Yes. But who arranged it so that the Israelites would encounter these fatigued—and edible—birds at just the right time? Coincidence . . . or God? The Bible is pretty clear about that.

The manna and the quail grew monotonous, as any food would, and later on the Israelites grumbled about their unvaried diet. On the other hand, it was much better than starving—or returning to slavery in Egypt. Later generations remembered the manna and praised God for it. He had promised Moses that he would provide for the people throughout their forty-year wilderness journey, and he did so.

The lesson of the miraculous food is nicely summed up in Deuteronomy 8:3: "He humbled you, causing you to hunger and then feeding you with manna, which neither you nor your fathers had known, to teach you that man does not live on bread alone but on every word that comes from the mouth of the LORD."

Unicorns? Really?

That amazing one-horned beast (whatever it was)

Do unicorns really exist? Of course they do . . . in that wonderful far-off place called Fantasyland. But oddly enough, you will find them in the Bible, too—or at least in the King James Version, published in 1611. That well-loved version mentions them several times. A few examples:

* God brought them out of Egypt; he hath as it were the strength of an unicorn. (Num. 23:22 KJV)

* His horns are like the horns of unicorns. (Deut. 33:17 KJV)

* Save me from the lion's mouth: for thou hast heard me from the horns of the unicorns. (Ps. 22:21 KJV)

* But my horn shalt exalt thee like the horn of an unicorn. (Ps. 92:10 KJV)

Hmmm. It appears that unicorns existed in Old Testament times. So maybe all those wonderful stories about unicorns existing, and then becoming extinct, are true. Right?

It's a pleasant thought, for even today people are enchanted with unicorns, the horse-like beasts that sport a single horn in the middle of the forehead. But the truth is, those old English scholars back in 1611 simply didn't know as much as they should have known about Hebrew. The Hebrew word they translated as "unicorn" was *re'em*, and it definitely did not refer to the mythical beast, but to some actual living creature. The scholars were on the right track, though: they knew that the Hebrew word was referring to something with horns—perhaps one horn, perhaps two.

Science hadn't progressed too far in those days, and much of the world was still unexplored. (Remember that it was 1611—just a few short years after the first Englishmen had set foot on North America.) For all those English translators knew, there really were unicorns somewhere in the world. *We* know unicorns are legendary—but they didn't.

In fact, they were following an established pattern. When the Old Testament was translated into Greek many centuries ago, the translators used the Greek word *monoceros*—"one horn." Later, the Latin translations used *unicornis*—meaning (yep!) "one horn." So when the King James translator opted for "unicorn," he was following an old tradition.

We have come a long way in our knowledge of Hebrew, too. Consider the four Bible verses quoted above, but this time in a few modern versions:

* God brings him out of Egypt, he is like the wild ox's horns to him. (Num. 23:22 JEB)

* His horns are the horns of a wild ox. (Deut. 33:17 NRSV)

* You have rescued me from the horns of the wild oxen. (Ps. 22:21 ESV)

* You have exalted my horn like that of a wild ox. (Ps. 92:10 NIV)

Notice a pattern here? Clearly a lot of contemporary translators think that the "unicorns" were really "wild oxen." They are probably right—but the translators would admit they are not 100 percent sure, for there is still some mystery about many of the ancient Hebrew words, particularly ones that refer to plants and animals.

Actually, one other alternative to *unicorn* is *rhinoceros*. It has one large horn (on the end of its nose, that is) and is a fearsome beast, one that might fit the verses we quoted earlier. And though it doesn't live in Israel today, it probably did in ancient times. Still, the translators tend to side with "wild ox."

"Wild ox" is likely more accurate than "unicorn"—but not nearly as picturesque. For hundreds of years, artists who painted biblical scenes had the pleasure of being able to put unicorns in their pictures, since the Bible (or the King James Version, anyway) said that unicorns existed. Go to an art museum and find a painting of the animals marching toward Noah's ark, and inevitably you will see unicorns in it.

While we're on the subject of mythical beasts, consider another one that appears in the Bible: the cockatrice. It isn't as well known as the unicorn, but in legend the cockatrice was a kind of serpent that could kill with a mere glance. The Bible mentions it in a few places, such as this verse from Isaiah: "And the sucking child shall play on the hole of the asp, and the weaned child shall put his hand on the cockatrice' den" (11:8 KJV). Well, we know what an "asp" is: the famous Egyptian cobra (the kind of snake Cleopatra used to commit suicide, remember?). We have no way of knowing whether the King James scholars actually believed that the fearsome cockatrice actually existed. But scholars today feel fairly certain that Isaiah 11:8 is referring to some venomous snake, so today's translations have "viper" or "adder."

Now, one more legendary creature: the satyr. In Greek mythology, satyrs were creatures of the woods and other wild places, creatures made like men from the waist up, like goats from the waist down, and also with the ears and horns of goats. Such beings never existed, of course, but satyrs appear twice in the King James Version, both times in Isaiah (13:21, 34:14). The Hebrew word that they translated as "satyr" referred to some shaggy creature of the wild, and today's translations have "wild goat" instead. Since the mythical satyrs were supposed to be half-goat, the King James translators had been half right.

There is no moral lesson in all this, but it is comforting to know that Bible translation is always getting better, with our knowledge of the ancient languages expanding all the time. The scholars who produced the King James Version in the 1600s did the best they could, but we have learned much since then. When you pick up any contemporary translation of the Bible, you can feel pretty confident that you are getting the real meaning of the original Hebrew and Greek.

The Prostitute's Son, and His Poor Daughter

The worst possible fate for an only child

W e're going to look at the career of a military leader named Jephthah, one of the great warriors of the Old Testament. But first we have to look at the whole concept of sacrifice, or you won't really appreciate Jephthah's story. Israel, like all the nations and tribes around it, had a religious system based on sacrifices. To your god you would give, or dedicate, something of value to you—a sheep, a goat, a bull, or a portion of your crops. The gods couldn't literally eat these goods, of course, and in practice some of what people sacrificed was used by the priests, and some by the person offering the sacrifice.

But Israel differed from its pagan neighbors in several ways, one being that the Israelites were horrified at the practice of sacrificing children. In another chapter in this book you can read more about the sacrifices of infants to the pagan god Molech. Israel's God did not ask his people to sacrifice humans, let alone children, to him, and God's prophets frequently condemned the Israelites who did sacrifice their infants.

It so happened that Molech was the god of the people known as the Ammonites, who were oppressing Israel at the time of Jephthah. So, as you read on, keep in mind that the Ammonites regularly sacrificed children to their god, and the Israelites found this appalling.

Now, to Jephthah. He lived in a place called Gilead, which also happened to be his father's name. His father had many sons by his wife, but Jephthah's mother was a prostitute. His half-brothers drove him off, wanting him to have no part in their father's inheritance. So Jephthah settled elsewhere and gathered around him a band of renegades and adventurers—nasty characters, probably, but at that time Israel desperately

94

needed some tough guys to fight off the Ammonites. Some of the people of Gilead begged him to come and deliver them.

Jephthah agreed, but first he tried diplomacy: he sent a letter asking the Ammonite chieftain why his people were oppressing Israel (see Judg. 11). The chieftain sent back a letter, claiming that centuries earlier the Israelites had taken Ammonite land, so now they were taking it back. (History repeats itself, doesn't it? In this same territory today, the various nations and ethnic groups are still squabbling over turf, still reminding each other of events that happened long, long ago.)

Jephthah sent back a reply: *You are wrong, Ammonite chief, and you are deliberately misreading the historical record.* But the Ammonite chief paid no attention to the message. The truth was, as in most situations like this, he simply enjoyed conquering and marauding for its own sake.

Since diplomacy failed, Jephthah had to use force (which, we have to admit, is usually the only thing that thugs like the Ammonite chieftain understand). Alas, in preparing to fight, Jephthah made a vow to the Lord: "If you give the Ammonites into my hands, whatever comes out of the door of my house to meet me when I return in triumph from the Ammonites will be the LORD's, and I will sacrifice it as a burnt offering" (Judg. 11:30).

Note that the Israelites, and all ancient peoples, took vows very seriously. A promise was a promise, no loopholes, no changing of the mind afterward. Jephthah had committed himself. Perhaps he assumed that the "whatever" that came out of his house would be some animal—a sheep or goat or calf. (In the ancient Middle East, of course, this happened all the time.)

The Lord was definitely with Jephthah. He took his men to the Ammonite territory, and they devastated twenty towns. "Thus Israel subdued Ammon" (Judg. 11:32).

Now, the sad part of this story:

> When Jephthah returned to his home in Mizpah, who should come out to meet him but his daughter, dancing to the sound of tambourines! She was an only child. Except for her he had neither son nor daughter. When he saw her, he tore his clothes and cried, "Oh! My

daughter! You have made me miserable and wretched, because I have made a vow to the LORD that I cannot break." (Judg. 11:34–35)

She was not only his only child, but an adorable one at that: instead of screaming or running away, she told her father to fulfill his vow just as he had promised. But she asked him one final request: give her two months to "roam the hills and weep with my friends, because I will never marry" (Judg. 11:37). Jephthah granted her request, and at the end of the two months she returned.

The writer of Judges was so horrified by what happened that he did not describe the sacrifice, but states only that Jephthah "did to her as he had vowed" (Judg. 11:39). What a bizarre twist of fate: Jephthah had defeated these people who were notorious for sacrificing their children in the fire—and the price he paid for his victory was sacrificing his daughter in the fire.

Jephthah is a truly tragic character. Obviously he was an intelligent man and a valiant warrior. But his vow to the Lord was rash, and he clearly did not think through his words before speaking them. As we said before, the Bible's people take vows seriously—not only the keeping of them, but the careful consideration of them beforehand. We can all learn a lesson here: don't make a promise to God without weighing it carefully, being sure you can keep it to the letter.

Sad as the story is, it has had universal appeal. Composer George Frederick Handel, famous for his oratorio *Messiah*, also wrote *Jephthah*, providing some superb music for one of the most heartrending stories in the whole Bible.

A Splitting (Literally) Headache

A spunky woman who really had her man pegged

The ancient world was a man's world, and by the standards of today most societies were sexist, with little concern for equal rights. So admittedly, women play a lesser role in the Bible than men do. But there are some notable and amazing women in its pages, and you see that especially in Judges 4–5, with two remarkable women named Deborah and Jael.

The author of Judges describes Deborah as both a "prophetess" (4:4) and "judge." She acted as a literal judge, holding court under the "Palm of Deborah," where people came to have her settle their disputes. (Before Judge Judy there was Judge Debbie.) She had enough clout to order an Israelite man named Barak to command a large army and fight against the oppressive Canaanites. Here's a surprise: Barak agreed to fight, but only if Deborah went with him.

Here's another surprise: Deborah agreed to go with him, but because of his request, she told him, the honor of winning the battle would not go to him but to a woman. He assumed, probably, that she was referring to herself, but that was not to be the case.

The commander of the Canaanite forces was Sisera, who had nine hundred iron chariots. A tough opponent, but Deborah was there to egg Barak on. He and his men fought well in the battle, with God's help, and not a Canaanite was left—except Sisera himself. He fled on foot and came to the tent of a woman named Jael. She was an Israelite, but there were, Judges says, "friendly relations" (4:17) between her family and the Canaanites, so Sisera assumed he would be treated well.

"Jael went out to meet Sisera and said to him, 'Come, my lord, come right in. Don't be afraid.' So he entered her tent, and she put a covering over him" (Judg. 4:18). She gave him something to drink and even agreed to stand in the opening of her tent so that if the Israelites came looking for him, she would lie and tell them he wasn't there.

But Jael was not as cooperative as Sisera thought. While he lay sleeping, exhausted from battle, she took a hammer and drove a tent peg through his temple—all the way into the ground, in fact. Barak came by, and Jael showed him his enemy—literally pinned to the ground.

Chapter 5 of Judges is the famous Song of Deborah, in which the woman judge praises both Barak and Jael, "most blessed of women" (v. 24). Deborah had prophesied right: the glory of the battle went to a woman.

Jael sounds like a sadistic lady, but the author of Judges didn't see it that way. Sisera was the leader of an army that had oppressed Israel for twenty years. Even though his soldiers were wiped out in that day's battle, had he lived he would have returned home and led more armies against Israel. Jael's act was bloody, but certainly excusable under the circumstances. As I note several times in this book, God moves in mysterious ways, and on this occasion, gory as it sounds to us, a woman with a tent peg and a mallet was doing the will of God.

Window to Heaven

Even the best preachers can put people to sleep . . .

History buffs know that the amazing "Stonewall" Jackson, Confederate general during the Civil War, was a devout Christian who prayed often and faithfully attended church whenever possible. Jackson loved to read the Bible and books of theology, but oddly enough, he always seemed to fall asleep during the sermon. One of his fellow generals lamented, "Why does Jackson bother going to church? He sleeps all the time!" Chalk it up to his frequent physical exhaustion, not to lack of interest. But then again, perhaps some of the preachers he heard were not that dynamic.

One of the great preachers of all time was, of course, the extremely dynamic apostle Paul, and happily we have many of his words recorded in the New Testament. Luke wrote the book of Acts (as well as the Gospel of Luke), and he was at times a missionary companion of Paul, so we can safely assume that Acts contains many of the actual utterances of Paul. Acts even tells us that on one dramatic occasion, Paul did manage to put a listener to sleep—with fatal results.

Acts 20 tells of Paul's sojourn in the city of Troas. If that name reminds you of the ancient city of Troy, that is appropriate, for Troas was in the same region as Troy, a district known as (surprise!) the Troad. In other words, Paul was in the very region where the great events of the epic poem *The Iliad* took place. But Paul had other things on his mind than Greek mythology: he was spreading the faith, teaching the true God instead of the false (and often immoral) gods of the Greek myths.

Acts notes that "on the first day of the week we came together to break bread." In other words, they were having church on Sunday, but as there were no church buildings as such, they met in believers' homes. (In fact, this is the first time the Bible mentions Sunday worship.) Paul had spent a week in Troas, and he knew he would be departing the following day, so like a good pastor he had lots to say to the people before he took leave of them. In fact, Acts says, he "kept on talking until midnight" (Acts 20:7).

People no doubt had longer attention spans in those days, and there was no precedent for Sunday worship being limited to only an hour or so. Many of these people were probably slaves or day laborers, and it is likely that they enjoyed their fellowship, so if the great apostle Paul wanted to speak to them into the late hours, that was fine.

The brothers were meeting in a third-story room, and a young man named Eutychus was seated in a window. Note: when you encounter the word *window* in the Bible, you can safely assume that it refers to an opening, not something with glass in it. In other words, Eutychus was seated on the wide sill of a third-story opening, with either his back or side to the ground below. "When he was sound asleep, he fell to the ground from the third story and was picked up dead" (Acts 20:9).

End of the Eutychus story? Not at all. "Paul went down, threw himself on the young man, and put his arms around him. 'Don't be alarmed,' he said. 'He's alive!'" Indeed he was. After this dramatic interruption, Paul kept on talking until daylight. "The people took the young man home alive and were greatly comforted" (Acts 20:10, 12). The name *Eutychus* means "fortunate," and never was a man truer to his name.

We know nothing else about Eutychus. If he was like most of the other early Christians, he worked hard at his labor and was probably tired. People in those days did not have weekends off from their jobs. This Christian meeting probably began after sundown, when work had ended, and Eutychus had likely put in a hard day's work.

A fall from a third-story window could easily kill a person, especially if the surface below was stone. Acts says that Eutychus was definitely dead when his friends first picked him up, and remember that Luke, "the physician" who wrote Acts, was actually present when this happened. We have no idea whether Eutychus was "clinically dead" or not. If he was, he was neither the first nor last case of a clinically dead person coming back to life. Acts doesn't dwell on the details much, and we aren't sure if Paul actually performed a miracle or if the young man simply wasn't as shattered as everyone thought. We can safely assume that his fellow Christians were grateful to God that the man survived a fall from a third-story window. It was a kind of "mini-resurrection," a reminder to the Christians that God brings the dead to life. In a sense Eutychus was, like Christ himself, a preview of the resurrection of all people of faith.

Jonah, the Runaway Prophet

New light on the world's oldest fish story

Alas, that controversial little book of the Old Testament, the book of Jonah. Only four brief chapters, but it has gotten attention way out of proportion to its length.

Think back to 1925. That was the year of the famous "Monkey Trial," the trial in which Tennessee schoolteacher John Scopes was taken to court because he taught the theory of evolution. The media at the time saw this as a grand opportunity to make Christians (and Southerners) look backward and foolish. The trial wasn't really Scopes versus Tennessee, but Secular Thought versus Traditional Christianity. Scopes lost the trial, but Secular Thought won . . . or so everyone believed.

One of the participants in the trial was politician William Jennings Bryan, who had served in the Senate, as Secretary of State, and as three-time Democratic presidential candidate. Bryan was also a committed Christian, and as he sat in the witness box, John Scopes's lawyer Clarence Darrow grilled him. The wily Darrow, very much the secular man, tried to make Bryan look foolish. He asked Bryan if he really believed the Bible when it stated that a whale swallowed Jonah. Bryan, who knew his Bible well, replied that, no, the Bible didn't say that at all: it said a "great fish" swallowed Jonah.

He was correct, but Darrow and his secular friends got a snicker out of the answer. Whether the culprit was a whale or a "great fish" didn't matter. To the "progressive" thinkers, Bryan and other people who seriously believed the Jonah story were a bunch of morons. After all, everyone *knows* a man can't survive inside a whale.

Well, the truth is, a man can, and it has been proven. (More about that in a moment.) But aside from that, the Bible is full of miracles, and if you can accept that miracles are possible, you can accept that Jonah might have survived inside the whale thanks to the power of God. If you can't accept miracles, well, you might as well stop reading the Bible, for its authors clearly did believe in a God who could, at certain times, choose to do out-of-the-ordinary things.

One obvious response to Clarence Darrow and all skeptics is this: it is true that, under normal circumstances, miracles do not occur, but they do at times. While it is hard to believe that a man could be swallowed by a whale, survive three days inside it, and then be vomited up on land, still alive, there is no reason this might not have happened on one occasion.

But there is another response to the skeptics, and that is the recorded account of a sailor named James Bartley. In February 1891 he was a crew member on the whaling ship *Star of the East*, which was in the waters off the Falkland Islands near South America. Bartley was one of several men let down in the longboats sent to pursue a sperm whale. One of the men harpooned the whale, which submerged itself, then suddenly surfaced, rocketing the men into the air. But after a long struggle the whale died, surfacing near the ship. The crew hoisted it alongside the ship, and began cutting it up into smaller pieces.

When the whale's stomach was hauled onto the deck, the crew noticed it was moving slightly. The ship's doctor cut the stomach open, and inside was James Bartley—curled up and unconscious, but still alive. He had been inside the whale for fifteen hours. The whale's digestive juices had removed all the hair from his body and bleached his skin white. Also, he was nearly blind. (Stomach acid is powerful stuff.)

It was nearly a month before James fully regained his senses. He recalled being shot into the air when the whale surfaced, falling into its open mouth, and being dragged across its teeth. Then he slid down the beast's esophagus and lost consciousness because of insufficient oxygen.

Here's an irony: it was his very first voyage on a whaler. It was also (this won't surprise you) his last one. After such a harrowing adventure, he had no taste for sea life. He settled down to life as a shoemaker in England. His tombstone there is inscribed "A Modern Jonah."

This isn't fiction. A whale swallowed a man, who survived fifteen hours inside it. According to the Bible, the prophet Jonah survived three days and nights inside the "great fish." And he was conscious, for chapter 2 of the book contains the prayer he uttered while inside the beast. Jonah was not cut out of the whale, as Bartley was, but was, the Bible says, "vomited out . . . upon the dry land" (Jon. 2:10 RSV).

In other words, the James Bartley story does not prove that the book of Jonah is true. It only proves that a human being can survive a short time inside a whale. Could anyone survive three whole days? We don't know. Again, if you believe in miracles, you would have to admit that perhaps God did indeed protect his prophet.

Back to the matter of terminology: the book of Jonah says the prophet was swallowed by a "great fish" (1:17). We know today that whales are mammals, meaning animals that give milk to their young. They are not even remotely related to fish. But the ancient Hebrews had not grown up reading *National Geographic* or watching the Discovery Channel. To their eyes, a sperm whale had fins and flippers and lived in the ocean, so it was a "great fish." And we know from the James Bartley story that a sperm whale can indeed swallow a person. If a sea creature really "ate" Jonah, it was most likely a sperm whale. Whether you choose to accept it as true or as an amusing story is a matter of faith.

People get distracted by the question—*Did he really get swallowed by a whale?*—and miss the bigger point of the story. God had told the prophet Jonah to go and preach repentance to the heathen city of Nineveh. Jonah had no desire to see wicked pagans repent so he sought to run away from God (fat chance) by taking a sea voyage.

Naturally you cannot run away from God. A storm struck the ship and everyone panicked. Jonah confessed to his fellow travelers that he knew why they were all in peril: it was because he had disobeyed God. Showing he had a good heart, he told the crew to hurl him into the sea—they did, "and the sea ceased from its raging" (Jon. 1:15 RSV). Jonah did not drown—he entered the belly of a "great fish" and lived to tell it.

This is the part of the story that people forget: the whale was not a punishment but was God's way of saving Jonah from drowning in the sea. Jonah had tried to run from his sacred duty. God could have let him die, but he did not. When Jonah made it alive out of the whale, he was willing to go and preach to Nineveh, as God had ordered.

It is a truly bizarre story, this tale of a reluctant prophet turned hors d'oeuvre for a whale. But readers ought to shift their attention from the whale to the God who provided the whale as a "life preserver." And we would all be wise to do our duty when God calls us, or we might learn, as Jonah did, that God is not easily avoided.

The Samson Angel,
Up in Smoke

———

Wouldn't stay for dinner, but was all fired up to leave

Can angels eat food? One angelic encounter (Abraham and the three visitors, Gen. 18) has them eating and drinking. On another occasion, an angel could not—or at least *would* not—eat the food its human hosts offered. That angel was connected with the birth of the hero Samson.

Judges 13 tells us that a man named Manoah had a wife who could not bear children, but an angel approached her and told her she would conceive, though she had to dedicate the child as a Nazirite. The wife told Manoah that "a man of God came to me. He looked like an angel of God, very awesome. I didn't ask him where he came from, and he didn't tell me his name" (v. 6).

Manoah himself wanted to see the angel, and he prayed to God to send him again. The angel returned, and Manoah asked it to stay for dinner—a dinner of young goat. The angel claimed he would not eat the food, nor tell Manoah his name, for "it is beyond understanding" (Judg. 13:18). He did tell Manoah he could offer up the young goat as a sacrifice to God, which Manoah did.

Then, the dramatic finish: "As the flame blazed up from the altar toward heaven, the angel of the LORD ascended in the flame. Seeing this, Manoah and his wife fell with their faces to the ground" (Judg. 13:20). So much for the images of the cute, cuddly angels that look liked winged infants.

"When the angel of the LORD did not show himself again to Manoah and his wife, Manoah realized that it was the angel of the LORD. 'We are doomed to die!' he said to his wife. 'We have seen God!'" (Judg.

13:21–22). His wife was calmer: if God had meant to kill them, he would not have accepted their sacrifice.

Most of us will never experience such dramatic encounters with the divine. This story is a colorful reminder for us that God is truly awesome.

The Daniel Diet

—

Young, handsome, healthy, and nonconformist

Diet and exercise, diet and exercise, diet and exercise—we talk about them so often that we ought to pause sometimes and ask, "Whatever did people converse about before everyone became obsessed with what they ate and how much they worked out?" Discussions of weight, cholesterol, calories, weight training, resistance training, and so on, are the red meat of our conversations these days.

This would have amazed our ancient ancestors. For most of human history, the basic rule was: eat whatever you can. The vast majority of humans who ever lived felt fortunate to have any food at all. They took what was available and made no fuss about whether it was low-fat, high-fat, cholesterol-free, or preservative-free. You don't have to read far in the Bible before you notice the word *famine* crops up often, and it has been a real threat throughout history. People who live in fear of famine do not have much fear of cholesterol or calories. Most of our ancestors would have fallen on the floor laughing at hearing the common complaint of today, "I really need to lose a few pounds."

It's true that the Bible does have some harsh words to say to the rich and gluttonous. The apostle Paul, writing to the Philippians, condemned people whose "god is their stomach" (3:19). The Hebrew prophets likewise condemned the idle rich who reclined on their ivory couches and made a hobby of eating and drinking—ignoring the many poor people who were literally starving. But rich people were a tiny minority in the ancient world.

If you watch religious TV or listen to religious radio, you probably notice that Christianity today has become very hip in terms of the diet-and-exercise obsession. Many Christian speakers and authors would

108

have you believe that God not only wants you healthy (a valid idea) but also wants you slim and youthful-looking (not necessarily a valid idea). Not everyone (this author included) agrees with that emphasis. The Bible does tell us that our total selves—our bodies included—belong to God, and thus we ought to take care of ourselves. But *taking care of* is not the same as *obsessing over*.

Do we really want a world where everyone is slim, athletic, and vigorous—"perfect"? Wasn't that the same kind of world Adolf Hitler wanted? Unless I seriously misread the New Testament, Christianity is all about transforming the *inner* person, becoming beautiful spiritually. There seems to be something amiss about a Christian group meeting together to rattle on about their calorie and cholesterol counts. Shouldn't we be more concerned about faith, hope, love, the fruits of the Spirit, love of God, and love of neighbor?

Having said all that, let's turn to the one episode in the Bible where diet became a central issue. It appears in the book of Daniel, which opens by telling of how Nebuchadnezzar, king of Babylon, had conquered Jerusalem and deported many of its citizens to Babylon. The king wisely decided to do what many conquerors do: take the really clever people from among the conquered and put them to work for himself. In doing so, the conqueror helped turn them to his own side.

So Nebuchadnezzar ordered his chief aide to bring in some of the Jewish upper crust—"young men without any physical defect, handsome, showing aptitude for every kind of learning, well informed, quick to understand, and qualified to serve in the king's palace" (Dan. 1:4). They were to learn the language and literature of the Babylonians. In short, these young men from the bumpkin little country of Judah were to be transformed culturally into Babylonians.

And they would learn to eat like Babylonians, too. "The king assigned them a daily amount of food and wine from the king's table. They were to be trained for three years, and after that they were to enter the king's service" (Dan. 1:5). Among these royal interns were Daniel and three of his friends.

To help nudge them into "going Babylonian," they received Babylonian names. Daniel was renamed *Belteshazzar*, and his three friends got names you have no doubt heard before: *Shadrach, Meshach,* and *Abednego*. It is appropriate that their Jewish names were changed, for all four of the young men had names that included the words *el* and *yah*—that is, "God" and "Lord." Daniel and his buddies received new "godless" names.

When your whole nation is conquered and you are shipped off to the capital of your conqueror, you generally do what you are told—or else. "But Daniel resolved not to defile himself with the royal food and wine, and he asked the chief official for permission not to defile himself this way" (Dan. 1:8). The chief official liked Daniel, so the book says, but he didn't like his request. He reminded Daniel that the king would have his head if Daniel ended up looking worse than the other royal interns.

So Daniel made a proposal: for ten days, give him and his three friends nothing but vegetables and water. Then compare their appearance with that of the other interns, the ones who were following the official diet. "At the end of the ten days they looked healthier and better nourished than any of the young men who ate the royal food. So the guard took away their choice food and the wine they were to drink and gave them vegetables instead" (Dan. 1:15–16).

God clearly approved of what these four had done, for he gave them knowledge and skill—and to Daniel he included the ability to interpret dreams and visions. At the end of the three-year internship, Daniel and his chums excelled above all the others in their abilities.

A quick note on "vegetables": the actual Hebrew word here means "seeds"—that is, cereal grains, such as wheat and barley. What Daniel and his friends were living on was not a vegetable-and-water diet but grains and water or bread and water.

The book rates the "Daniel diet"—vegetables and water—very highly. Meaning that the author of the book was recommending this diet to his readers? Probably not. He didn't need to, for probably most of them would have been on a diet of vegetables and water anyway—not by choice, but by necessity. There is a kind of underlying message here: *Be satisfied with your meager diet, for the faithful Daniel and his friends fared well on it, prospering more than the ones who ate the rich foods of the Babylonians.*

Note that the book says Daniel did not wish to "defile" himself with the royal diet. In our way of looking at things today, one can "defile" himself by taking in too much cholesterol, too many calories, too much fat. That isn't the kind of defilement Daniel was trying to avoid. Probably the Babylonian diet included foods that were nonkosher—that is, foods that the Jews were forbidden to eat, such as pork and shellfish.

Also, there was that ancient practice of sacrificing meat to pagan gods before eating it, something that faithful Jews wished to avoid. The kosher laws that Jews lived by applied only to meats, not grains, fruits, and vegetables, so Daniel's vegetarian diet was safe, religiously speaking. In short, the book of Daniel isn't any kind of plea for a vegetarian diet. It is making the case for holding to one's religious standards and not being pressed into the mold of a pagan culture.

A logical question does arise: why did Daniel and his friends appear healthier after ten days of bread and water? We don't know. We have no idea what they had been eating before that time. We can't rule out the possibility of a miracle—that God blessed the appearance of the four faithful young men who would not defile themselves with the pagans' food. We also can't rule out the possibility that they looked better because of their attitude—pleased with the knowledge they were adhering to their own dietary laws, and thus pleasing God.

The story has an obvious moral, and it certainly isn't *Be a vegetarian*. The moral is spiritual, not physical: When placed in a culture that is hostile to your own values and morals, stand firm. Don't just give in and conform. Daniel and his friends took a stand, and they fared well. So can we.

The Syrian Skin Man

Nothing like Israelite dirt for whatever ails you

The mighty prophet Elisha is one of the "biggies" of the Old Testament, a man remembered not only for taking a bold stand for God but for performing numerous miracles. One of his many miracles involved a foreign army man—proof that the God of Israel was also the God of the whole world, and that the distress of a foreign soldier did not escape his notice.

The soldier's name was Naaman, and he was commander of the army of Aram. Some Bible versions have "Syria" instead of "Aram"—same country, though, and one that was often at war with Israel in those days. Naaman suffered from what the Bible calls "leprosy"—which in those days could refer to the loathsome and disfiguring disease known as leprosy, or a hundred other chronic skin afflictions.

The Lord moves in mysterious ways. Naaman's army had captured a young girl of Israel, and she became a maid to Naaman's wife. The girl had every good reason to hate her captors, of course, but in fact she had a compassionate streak. "She said to her mistress, 'If only my master would see the prophet who is in Samaria! He would cure him of his leprosy'" (2 Kings 5:3). Naaman's wife told Naaman, who told the king of Aram, who gave Naaman leave to go to Israel to seek out the miracle man. Naaman didn't go empty-handed: he carried with him a huge load of gold and silver. He also carried a letter from his own king to the king of Israel.

The king of Israel (whom, for some odd reason, the Bible does not name) didn't understand the situation at all. He went into a tailspin, thinking that *he* was supposed to cure Naaman's skin disease. Elisha heard the king was in a dither, so he sent the king word to send Naaman on to him.

Naaman arrived at Elisha's home and received some odd instructions: "Go, wash yourself seven times in the Jordan, and your flesh will be restored and you will be cleansed" (2 Kings 5:10). Naaman was furious. He expected the prophet to perform a cure instantly, and with a lot of spectacle. And those instructions about washing in that pitiful creek they called the "river" Jordan—didn't his homeland have its own rivers for washing in? Naaman was angry, but his servant calmed him down. Why not give the prophet's orders a try? Couldn't hurt, could it?

"So he went down and dipped himself in the Jordan seven times, as the man of God had told him, and his flesh was restored and became clean like that of a young boy." Amazing what faith can do—or, more accurately, what God can do. Naaman was relieved—and impressed. He returned to Elisha and told him, "Now I know that there is no God in all the world except in Israel" (2 Kings 5:14–15). He wanted to give Elisha the silver and gold he had brought with him, but Elisha would not accept. God's prophets do not heal people in order to make money.

Naaman made a request: could he please carry away as much soil as a pair of mules could haul? Soil, you say? Sure. Naaman wanted some of the soil of Israel to take back with him. Most people in those days had a "localized" view of the gods. Israel's God had healed Naaman in Israel. So he wished to take some earth back so he could literally worship God on God's own soil.

Put another way, when he returned to Aram, he couldn't be sure the God of Israel would hear his prayers from there. We know better, of course—God is everywhere. But Naaman shared all the prejudices and superstitions of his day. He was grateful to this God of Israel and wanted to thank him often, so he wanted a "little piece of Israel" to take home with him so that this God would hear his prayers.

Naaman had another request of Elisha: please forgive him, for in the future he would have to pay his respects in the temple of his own god, Rimmon. In other words, Naaman was telling Elisha that his true god was now the God of Israel, but that he would have to go through the motions of worshiping Rimmon—out of a sense of official duty, that is. Elisha told him, "Go in peace" (2 Kings 5:19).

Elisha and Naaman both look good in this odd and charming story.

The one person who does not is Elisha's servant, Gehazi. He felt his master was a fool for not accepting the lavish gifts Naaman had offered. So after Naaman departed, he ran after him and told him a lie: his master did need some of the money after all. Naaman happily gave him what he asked, and Gehazi returned home with his loot—not bothering to tell Elisha, naturally.

Gehazi had underestimated his master. Elisha asked where he had been, and Gehazi lied and said, "Nowhere." Elisha was not fooled: "Was not my spirit with you when the man got down from his chariot to meet you?" Somehow, miraculously, Elisha had seen it all. And Gehazi got his comeuppance, for Elisha told him, "Naaman's leprosy will cling to you and your descendants forever." As he had spoken so it was: Gehazi became leprous, "as white as snow" (2 Kings 5:26–27).

Many people react with horror to the last part of this story. Wasn't Elisha being a bit harsh? Maybe. But consider what had happened: a foreigner, a soldier in the army of an enemy nation, a worshiper of idols, had come to Elisha for a cure. He had been cured, praising Israel's God. Elisha wasn't about to mar this wonderful event by accepting payment for it. Divine love and power were not for sale. Gehazi had turned a compassionate miracle into a "deal." Elisha's curse on him was a reminder: we don't do works of compassion for gain.

Raising the Roof (Literally)

The lengths (and heights) people would go to for healing

People today are pretty skeptical about miracles, which is why the modern mind tends to remember Jesus as the wise teacher, not the miracle worker. But he was both, and you see this very clearly in Mark's Gospel. Mark doesn't contain as much of Jesus' teaching as the other Gospels, but it is full to the brim with miracles, one after another.

We learn in Mark 2 that Jesus was in the town of Capernaum, a kind of hub of his ministry, so much so that Mark calls it Jesus' "home," even though all the Gospels make it clear that he traveled a lot. When he returned to Capernaum on this occasion, "so many gathered that there was no room left, not even outside the door, and he preached the word to them" (vv. 1–2).

Some were there for the preaching, but others were there because of Jesus' reputation as a healer. "Some men came, bringing to him a paralytic, carried by four of them. Since they could not get him to Jesus because of the crowd, they made an opening in the roof above Jesus and after digging through it, lowered the mat the paralyzed man was lying on" (Mark 2:3–4).

This puzzles many Bible readers, since cutting a hole in the roof sounds like a major demolition job—not to mention upsetting the owner of that home, whoever it was. But the historians and archaeologists assure us that the typical homes in that time and place weren't much like our homes today. Possibly the house had a flat roof made of a thick layer of hardened (and packed-down) clay. Or even easier to cut through was the roof made of matting covered over with earth and twigs, and supported by rafters. Either way, the house would have had an outside stairway, which is how the men carrying the paralytic got up to the roof. And either way, cutting through would not have been too difficult.

Jesus did not stop to give these men a stern lecture on property rights. He saw something admirable in their cutting through the roof: they desperately wanted their friend healed, and they believed Jesus could do it. So, even though the house probably got a little dustier because of what happened, the story has a happy ending: Jesus told the man to get up, pick up his mat, and go home. "He got up, took his mat and walked out in full view of them all. This amazed everyone and they praised God, saying, 'We have never seen anything like this!'" (Mark 2:12).

Neither have most of us. Miracles of healing still do occur, although the extreme skeptics doubt them all. We don't know how Jesus healed the man, nor what caused the man's paralysis. We only know that the man's friends believed Jesus possessed the power to heal, and Jesus was pleased at their faith. Perhaps there are fewer miracles today because there is not much faith.

Call Him "Hash" for Short

What's in a name, especially the longest one?

In the Bible, names are serious business. When you gave a child a name, you didn't do so just because it sounded pretty, or because some friend or relative had that name. You picked the name because of its *meaning*. The name would, you hoped, reflect well on the person bearing it. And with many names, you hoped they would reflect well on God.

You've probably noticed that many Old Testament names contain an *-el* or an *-iah*. The *-iah* (or sometimes *-jah*) was the Hebrew word *Yah*, the name for God. (*Yah* was the short form of the full name for God, *Yahweh*.) *El* was the Hebrew word meaning "God." So every name with *-iah* or *-el* has some meaning relating to God. Zechariah means "*Yah* remembers." Daniel means "*El* [God] is judge." Elijah combines both names: "*Yah* is God." In short, many of the characters in the Bible had very godly names. They didn't always live up to them, but at least their parents had good intentions.

One man who did live up to his name was Isaiah ("*Yah* saves"). In Isaiah 8 we learn of the peculiar naming, and conception, of Isaiah's son: the Lord told Isaiah to write on a scroll the name *Maher-Shalal-Hash-Baz*. Then Isaiah went to his wife (called "the prophetess" in verse 3), and she conceived a son. When it was born, Isaiah bestowed on it the cumbersome name he had written on the scroll.

The Hebrew name *Maher-Shalal-Hash-Baz* means "speed-spoil-hasten-plunder"—that is, "quick to the plunder, swift to the spoils." God explained to Isaiah why the child would bear this bizarre name: "Before the child knows how to say 'My father' or 'My mother,' the wealth of

117

Damascus and the plunder of Samaria will be carried off by the king of Assyria" (Isa. 8:3–4).

In other words, the child's name was a bit of good news: the Assyrian empire would plunder the enemy cities of Damascus and Samaria. Throughout his life (the prophecy did come true) the child's name would be a reminder to the people of Judah that God protected them, and that he could use one warlike nation (Assyria) to do harm to other warlike nations.

The name *Maher-Shalal-Hash-Baz* is, as you might guess, the longest name in the Bible. Perhaps people called him *Maher* for short—which would have meant, roughly, "Speedy."

Isaiah was not the only prophet God commanded to give his children symbolic names. He ordered the prophet Hosea to marry a wayward woman with the name Gomer (yes, really). Among the children she bore him was a daughter named *Lo-Ruhamah*, meaning "not loved," for God decreed that the faithless kingdom of Israel was no longer loved. A son of Hosea was named *Lo-Ammi*, meaning "not my people," for God saw that the idol-worshiping Israelites were no longer his people.

If all this sounds terribly harsh, God made a promise to Hosea: sometime in the future, change would come, and instead of being cast off, the people of Israel would be called "sons of the living God" (Hos. 1:10). But as long as Hosea's children lived, their names were painful reminders: if the people did not love and honor God, they would no longer be his people.

We have to mention the three daughters of Job. You recall that poor Job was the wealthy man who suffered every possible calamity, yet still clung to God. Among his many tribulations were the deaths of all of his children, who all died when a mighty storm struck the house where they were feasting. But at the end of the book, the faithful Job had his fortunes restored. Though his children were dead, he and his wife had more children—ten sons and three daughters.

Normally the Bible regards sons as more worthy of attention than daughters, but the last chapter of Job breaks that pattern, for the seven sons are not named, while the three daughters are. Their names are *Jemimah*, *Keziah*, and *Keren-Happuch*—that is, "dove," "cassia" (a spice), and "jar of eye shadow" (no, we're not kidding). After learning their names, we learn why they are mentioned while the sons' names are not:

"Nowhere in all the land were there found women as beautiful as Job's daughters, and their father granted them an inheritance along with their brothers" (Job 42:15).

That last item is important: normally daughters did not inherit property, but Job was so wealthy that he gave his three beautiful daughters a legacy.

We can't conclude this chapter on names without stating the obvious: people of faith ought to give a little thought to the naming of their own children. Some names are pretty, and at any given time certain names are trendy, but giving a child a name with a spiritual meaning is always a good choice, particularly if the Bible character with that name was a good role model. The Bible offers many fine choices—though if you choose to pass up Maher-Shalal-Hash-Baz, no one would mind.

Old Sol, Stopped Dead in Its Tracks

The amazing Joshua, and a literally timeless battle

In our day of jumbo jets and interstate highways, distance is never a huge concern. Many people think nothing of driving fifty miles to their job in the morning, and so we find it very quaint that when our distant ancestors spoke of "a day's journey," they weren't talking about a huge distance. In ancient times, you traveled by camel, donkey, mule, or horse—or a vehicle pulled by these animals. But more likely, you just walked.

If you look at a map of the world, you see that Israel and Egypt are neighbors today. Israel is a relatively tiny country, and Egypt sits on its southwestern edge. In the early books of the Bible there was no "land of Israel," for the territory that became Israel was then called Canaan. It was to Canaan that the Israelite slaves were bound after God freed them from their bondage in Egypt. It took them forty years to get to Canaan. Read that again: *forty years* to get from Egypt to Canaan.

You may be scratching your head by now. Even allowing for the fact that they walked the entire route, and that it was a huge mass of people involved, and that marauders like the Amalekites waylaid them at times—still, forty years?

They took this much time for the obvious reason: God wanted it that way. This sounds almost cruel to us. These people had been slaves in Egypt, so why didn't God, after he freed them, make the trip to Canaan as brief as possible? But if you ask that question, maybe you don't know much about human nature. All the Israelites had been slaves. They were accustomed to being ordered about by their Egyptian masters. Their lives were harsh, but predictable. These people were not ready to govern themselves and to build an orderly, civil society. So the forty years served as a kind of political prep school.

In the Bible, *forty years* was another way of saying "one generation." The generation of slaves that left Egypt gradually died off, and children were born along the way. So the band that arrived in Canaan was not exactly the same band of slaves that left Egypt. They had learned some lessons along the way about being their own people, governing and ordering themselves, and also depending on God.

The book of Joshua, which needs to be studied more than it is, is all about the Israelites' conquest of Canaan. The land was already inhabited, and needless to say, the dwellers there did not exactly extend a warm welcome to this horde of people coming in from the desert, these "children of Israel," as they called themselves. But the Canaanites, who dwelt in walled villages and considered themselves much more civilized than the Israelites, learned something quickly: these desert people were pretty darned organized, and they knew how to fight. What the Canaanites did not know was that God was on the Israelites' side. They would learn, as the Egyptians had, that it was not wise to oppose Israel.

In Joshua 10 we read about the clash at Gibeon, a key battle that pitched Israel against the Canaanite people known as Amorites. (At that time the Amorites held the city called Jerusalem, the city that would eventually be the capital of Israel.) Joshua and his men marched to face the Amorites after God assured him that "not one of them will be able to withstand you" (v. 8). The Israelites marched all night and launched a surprise attack. The Amorites faced not only the Israelites' swords, but also hailstones—which God provided. The Bible notes that more died from the hailstones than from the Israelite swords.

But the hailstones were not the most miraculous occurrence that day. Something even more bizarre happened:

> On the day the LORD gave the Amorites over to Israel, Joshua said to the LORD in the presence of Israel:
> "O sun, stand still over Gibeon,
> O moon, over the Valley of Aijalon."
> So the sun stood still,
> and the moon stopped,
> till the nation avenged itself on its enemies,

as it is written in the Book of Jashar. The sun stopped in the middle of the sky and delayed going down about a full day. (Josh. 10:12–13)

Skeptics read this and say "Poppycock!" Even people who believe in miracles have a hard time with this particular one. God made time stand still? Really? Wasn't it more likely a case of the participants in the battle *feeling* that time stood still for them? That has happened to everyone, hasn't it, in the middle of some intense experience?

Some Bible scholars claim that the Hebrew word that we translate as "stand still" can also mean "stop shining." That is, the command was not for the sun to stop, but to darken—in other words, an eclipse. Possible? Maybe.

We are wiser today about astronomy, and we know the sun does not literally move across the sky (even though we still say that it sets and rises). If the sun really did appear to stand still, that could mean only that the whole earth literally stopped turning for a while. To us that is simply impossible, but the Israelites would not have seen it that way. God was in control of nature, and if he wished to make time stop on one occasion, well, he could do so.

The fact is, we have no idea what really happened at Gibeon, except that the Israelites defeated the Amorites, and they gave the credit to God. In the book of Joshua, with many accounts of amazing victories in battles, the battle of Gibeon stands out.

Note that a certain "Book of Jashar" is mentioned as the source for the story of the sun standing still. The Old Testament refers to that book in a couple of other places, and all we know is that it was a very ancient book, one that the Old Testament authors drew upon when writing history.

Joshua mentioned the book for an obvious reason: it was the author's way of saying, "Look, I'm not making all this up, I'm basing it on an old and respected source, the Book of Jashar." This was one of several places in the Bible where its authors paused to say to the reader, "Hey, you can trust us."

Gray-Bearded Cheerleader

Gooooooo, Israelites! Go!

If you ever saw the original *Star Wars*, you might recall those unattractive people called the Tusken Raiders, also known as the Sand People. The scriptwriters clearly modeled these on the Bedouin, the various nomadic tribes that lived, and still live, in the desert regions of the Middle East and northern Africa. Like the fictional Tusken Raiders, the Bedouin have their own distinctive moral code, which does not rule out preying on other tribes and people that happen to come their way. They live by herding sheep, goats, and camels—and by stealing from unwary travelers.

Some things are timeless, for such people existed at the time the Israelites made their long trek from Egypt to Canaan. It would be a gross understatement to say that they were a thorn in Israel's side.

Among these nomadic tribes was a group known as the Amalekites. They inhabited the vast area between Egypt and Canaan, and since they were nomads, they had no real capital or "center" to their tribal lands. Genesis says they were descendants of Esau, the brother of Jacob, so the Israelites regarded them as distant kin, but there was no family love at all between them. The Israelites encountered them fairly soon after leaving Egypt, as we learn in Exodus 17. In fact, they were the first (but certainly not the last) group of people to make war on Israel in its post-Egyptian days.

> The Amalekites came and attacked the Israelites at Rephidim. Moses said to Joshua, "Choose some of our men and go out to fight the Amalekites. Tomorrow I will stand on top of the hill with the staff of God in my hands."

So Joshua fought the Amalekites as Moses had ordered, and Moses, Aaron and Hur went to the top of the hill. (Exod. 17:8–10)

Why did the Amalekites attack? They didn't need a reason. The Israelites were on a journey, and that meant they carried possessions with them. The Amalekite nomads saw these new people as a source of plunder. Aside from that, they may simply have seen the Israelites as intruders, and in ancient times, the usual assumption was "If we don't know them, they must be bad."

Note that the character Joshua is part of this story, and this is the first time the Bible mentions him. He was sort of young assistant to Moses and as we learn in later books of the Bible, he took Moses' place as leader of Israel once Moses had passed on. Joshua is introduced rather abruptly here, as if the people reading this story would say, "Ah, yes—the famous Joshua!" Clearly Moses respected Joshua's fighting ability.

Remember that in their liberation from Egypt, the Israelites had never relied in any way on human force. It was God who sent the ten plagues on the Egyptians, and though Moses played a role, he was nothing more than God's spokesman. Now that they were in the desert, the Israelites continued to rely on God for their provisions of food. But they did not, as this passage shows, sit back and wait for God to fight off their attackers. They may have believed God was on their side, but that didn't keep them from taking up their swords when the time came.

Moses himself did not fight. He and his brother Aaron went up to a hill to watch the battle. He did more than just watch, however. The mighty man of God also played the role of the Israelites' cheerleader:

As long as Moses held up his hands, the Israelites were winning, but whenever he lowered his hands, the Amalekites were winning. When Moses' hands grew tired, they took a stone and put it under him and he sat on it. Aaron and Hur held his hands up—one on one side, one on the other—so that his hands remained steady till sunset. (Exod. 17:11–12)

And apparently this "cheerleading" pose was effective, for "Joshua overcame the Amalekite army with the sword" (Exod. 17:13).

How are we to interpret this passage? Was there some kind of magical power in Moses having his arms up? Of course not. There is nothing in this story to indicate that anything miraculous took place. It is pretty clear that the sight of their leader on the hill with his arms raised in the air strengthened the Israelite men—the same way many soldiers in battle draw strength from seeing their flag waving. Moses on the hill was a sort of combination of cheerleader and tribal flag. Moses himself must have been thinking of a flag, for after the Israelite victory, he set up an altar and gave it a name: "The LORD is my banner" (Exod. 17:15).

Keep this in mind: Moses was not empty-handed there on the hill, for, as he told Joshua, he was holding "the staff of God"—that is the same rod that was associated with several miracles, including the turning of the river of Egypt to blood. The staff itself was not magical, of course, but the Israelites naturally connected it with the power of God.

The Israelite fighting men in the thick of battle could not see the invisible God, but they could see Moses, and they could see his staff—a simple piece of wood, yes, but something they linked with divine aid. Later on, Israel would have the famous ark of the covenant as a visible reminder of God's presence, but for now, Moses' staff served that purpose. Moses the "cheerleader" had something much better than a "pom-pom."

We don't know exactly why, but for some reason God placed a kind of curse on the Amalekites: "Then the LORD said to Moses, 'Write this on a scroll as something to be remembered and make sure that Joshua hears it, because I will completely blot out the memory of Amalek from under heaven'" (Exod. 17:14). The curse did not take hold immediately, for the Amalekites were still giving Israel trouble during the time of the judges, and even during the reign of King David. But finally, in the reign of Hezekiah, the remaining Amalekites are said to have been completely destroyed (see 1 Chron. 4:43).

The Amalekites, nasty folk though they were, were not the main point of this story. The point was that this was Israel's first battle with a foe, and they prevailed. God had helped them before and would do so again, but they had learned that at times they needed to rally their own human strength. That is a valid lesson for us today, and so is the example of Moses on the hill, a reminder that some people can, simply by their presence, make a huge difference.

As Old as . . .
You Know Who

—

Amazing longevity, and without doctors, diets, or health clubs

Skeptics like to point out that the Bible has a lot in common with the writings of other ancient religions. There are flood stories through-out the world, and all of them bear some resemblance to the Noah story in the Bible. This doesn't, contrary to what the skeptics say, prove anything. Actually it hints that the Bible story is correct, based on a truth that got distorted and mangled in other religions.

Another example: old Babylonian records show lists of kings—and some of them (so the records say) lived more than a thousand years. Sound familiar? Sure it does—sounds like Genesis 5, that long list of names that includes the remarkable Methuselah, who lived to be (gasp!) 969 years. Wow. Second in longevity was Jared, who died relatively young—only 962 years. And if you bother to read Genesis 5, you'll note that the first man himself, old Adam, died at the ripe age of 930. His son Seth lived to be 912, and Seth's son Enosh lived to be 905.

Bizarre (and perhaps unbelievable) as these figures seem to us, the most bizarre item in Genesis 5—and also the most inspiring—is what it says of Enoch: "Enoch walked with God; then he was no more, because God took him away" (v. 24). Where? To heaven, we assume. That is surely more important than the fact that Enoch was the father of Methuselah. The mention of God's "taking" Enoch was the Bible's first hint that there may be an afterlife.

Back to that longevity business: are these numbers possible? Why not? Maybe righteous living had its reward. The author of Genesis certainly thought so, for chapter 6 dives into a discussion of man's in-creasing wickedness, and God established 120 years as the normal life span. Centuries later, one of the Psalms would state that the normal span

126

was "threescore years and ten" (Psa. 90:10 KJV)—seventy, that is, not too far from our figure today.

The Old Testament definitely holds up long life as a thing to be desired. We don't find that attitude in the New Testament, however. What gripped the Christians was their strong belief in eternal life—and also the strong possibility of martyrdom. Dying young was no disgrace to the Christians; it just meant getting an early start on eternity.

Even so, the lesson of Genesis 5 is still valid: righteousness has its rewards. We view those rewards differently than the author of Genesis: instead of a long, long, *long* earthly life, the righteous can look forward to one that never ends.

Fleecing the Lord

Gideon, the very sheepish skeptic

E ver heard the expression "laying out the fleece"? People don't use it much anymore, but it referred to the testing of someone to find out if he was genuine. The phrase is based on the Bible's story of one of Israel's most famous military men—who was also a real skeptic at times.

This was Gideon, a farmer who became one of the judges of Israel. Elsewhere in this book we noted that "judges" is hardly the right name for these men, who would be more properly called "heroes" or "military leaders." They played the important role of delivering Israel from its various enemies, the many pagan tribes and nations on its borders.

Ever since they settled in Canaan following the long journey out of Egyptian slavery, the Israelites had problems with the locals. This was typical of ancient times—or come to think of it, of human history in general. Nations and tribes were always at war, and there was no talk of "diversity" or "tolerance" or "Can't we all just get along?" It was always a matter of survival of the fittest—or the most aggressive.

Under Joshua, the Israelites had settled in Canaan and displaced the people already there—but not completely. Some of the natives always remained, and their gods and religions (and low morals) were always a temptation to the Israelites. If you wonder why God allowed these immoral pagans to remain, Judges 2:22–23 explains it quite well. God says, " 'I will use them to test Israel and see whether they will keep the way of the LORD and walk in it as their forefathers did.' The LORD had allowed these nations to remain; he did not drive them out at once by giving them into the hands of Joshua." So the pagans were a way of trying out the Israelites' morality and devotion to God. This test they often failed.

In Judges 6, however, it was not the locals who were the problem but the marauders known as Midianites. "Because the power of Midian was so oppressive, the Israelites prepared shelters for themselves in mountain clefts, caves and strongholds" (Judg. 6:2). The Midianites were like a plague of locusts, coming in swiftly and carrying off everything the Israelites possessed. The people cried out to the Lord for help, and he heard them.

Gideon, for fear of the oppressive Midianites, was threshing wheat— not out in the open, but in a winepress. An angel came and greeted him: "The LORD is with you, mighty warrior." Here was one of many instances in the Bible where an angel appeared no different from any other human. Gideon certainly did not see a white-robed figure with wings in front of him. His reply to the angel had a bit of sarcasm in it: "If the LORD is with us, why has all this happened to us? . . . The LORD has abandoned us and put us into the hand of Midian" (Judg. 6:12–13). The angel wasn't one to mince words: he ordered Gideon to go and save Israel.

Gideon was skeptical—about himself, about his own family, and about this mysterious visitor. Was this messenger from God, as it seemed? While the angel waited, Gideon went and prepared a goat stew and some bread. He brought them out to the angel and set them on a rock. The angel touched the food with his staff. "Fire flared from the rock, consuming the meat and the bread. And the angel of the LORD disappeared" (Judg. 6:21). Gideon then knew he had been conversing with God's messenger.

Yet Gideon still doubted whether he could lead Israel's armies to defeat the Midianites. He wanted to know that God was really with him. He laid out a fleece on the ground and told God to give him a sign: if, the next morning, the fleece was wet and the ground around it was dry, he would believe. God did so, and Gideon wrung out a bowlful of water from the fleece. Then he asked God to do just the opposite: at night, leave the fleece dry but make the ground around it wet with dew. God did, and Gideon finally believed.

The skeptic proved to be one of the greatest military leaders in Israel's history. In the contest of Gideon versus Midian, Gideon prevailed. He honored God, and when the Israelites offered to make Gideon their king, he would not accept. God alone was Israel's king.

Gideon is an admirable character, though some would say he was way too doubtful. His initial encounter with the angel, in which fire consumed the food on the rock, would have been enough to convince most people that they had met with the power of God. It wasn't enough for Gideon, who posed not one but two more tests for God (the two involving the fleece, that is).

But Judges doesn't judge Gideon harshly for this. He had doubts about his own ability, and about the ability of Israel to fight off its powerful enemies. He was the type of person who had skill but simply needed some reassurance from an authority figure—who in this case was the ultimate Authority of all. Obviously God would prefer that we be consistently faithful and never doubtful of his power and love. But, as the Gideon story shows, he is at times accommodating to our human weaknesses.

Hot Pillar, Smoky Pillar

———

A column of ex-slaves following the column of God

A bit of trivia from the days of the American Revolution: the great scientist and patriot Benjamin Franklin proposed in 1776 that the new nation should adopt a national seal—specifically, an image of Moses leading the Israelites through the Red Sea. Franklin's friend Thomas Jefferson had another suggestion, also drawn from the Bible: the seal would show Israel being led through the wilderness by a pillar of fire. Both men saw the American Revolution as a kind of "exodus," a liberation from the oppressive nation of Great Britain.

Neither suggestion was adopted, though the proposals are interesting because they tell us that people in those days were very familiar with the Bible. Franklin and Jefferson were not practicing Christians but deists, yet they were both fond of the Bible and knew it had a hold on the American people. They were probably correct in assuming that every American at that time would immediately understand an image of the Israelites crossing the Red Sea, or being led by a pillar of fire.

Well, even today quite a few people are familiar with God parting the Red Sea so the Israelites could pass over it (and then releasing the waters so that the Egyptian troops were drowned). But what about the pillar of fire?

Exodus 13 tells about the Israelite ex-slaves setting forth from Egypt. They knew they were headed toward their ancestral homeland in Canaan, and they had the vague feeling that this land was north and east of Egypt. Beyond that, they knew nothing. They had no maps or compasses (no Global Positioning System, of course), and certainly no hope that the lands they were passing through would happily provide them with directions and other aid. So they had to rely on their only resource, God.

> By day the LORD went ahead of them in a pillar of cloud to guide them on their way and by night in a pillar of fire to give them light, so that they could travel by day or night. Neither the pillar of cloud by day nor the pillar of fire by night left its place in front of the people. (Exod. 13:21–22)

The pillar of cloud was more than just a guide when the Israelites were moving forward. It was also the signal for them to settle down to camp, or to move on. Once the Israelites had constructed the Tent of Meeting (or Tent of Testimony in some translations), the large tent (or tabernacle) that was the center of their worship life, the divine cloud became attached to the tent.

> Whenever the cloud lifted from above the Tent, the Israelites set out; wherever the cloud settled, the Israelites encamped . . . Whether the cloud stayed over the tabernacle for two days or a month or a year, the Israelites would remain in camp and not set out; but when it lifted, they would set out. (Num. 9:17, 22)

It's a lovely image, isn't it? This huge mass of people heading up through the wilderness, following a "pillar of cloud" by day and a "pillar of fire" by night. But the obvious question arises: what exactly were these two "pillars"?

The most obvious answer, but the one least acceptable to people today, is that they were just what the text suggests: a column of cloud and a column of fire, miraculously provided by God, who had no reason to explain to the Israelites just what these divine guides were made of. In some mysterious way God provided a visual phenomenon that the people could see both by day or night. The pillar of fire by night is particularly remarkable, for in ancient times, travel usually ceased at sunset, particularly in this situation where these people were trekking through an area they did not know, and where a false step at night might very well send them off a cliff.

Skeptics of the miraculous have suggested that the "pillar of cloud by day" sounds like a desert whirlwind. It does, and there is the possibility that God could have stirred up a whirlwind and sent it ahead of the Israelites for the purpose of guiding them. But a whirlwind would not be visible at night and would certainly not appear to be a "pillar of fire."

Skeptics have offered another suggestion: at the head of the Israelites marched some men carrying a smoking pot, which would be seen as smoke, or cloud, by day, and as a fire by night. It sounds plausible, but it leaves us with that nagging question: how did these men know where they were going, unless God showed them the way? And if God was somehow guiding them on, well, that is no less miraculous than his providing a "pillar of cloud" and "pillar of fire." So we are pretty much stuck with a choice: accept that God provided these peculiar visual guides, or say that the author of Exodus just invented the whole thing.

Clearly the book wants us to understand this much: the pillars symbolized God's presence among the people. The Israelites had just left the land of Egypt, with its numerous idols of its numerous gods. Those idols showed the gods in various forms—human, but more often half-human and half-animal, such as the god Anubis, with a man's body and a jackal's head. Israel's God would soon make it very clear in his Ten Commandments that Israelites must *not* ever make idols or bow down to them. God was with them, yes—but he was invisible, and they must never try to "localize" him by making any kind of image of him.

So there are no "pictures" of God in the Bible, yet there are occasionally signs of his presence. In the years of journeying through the wilderness to Canaan, the most common sign of God's presence was either a cloud or fire. Consider Exodus 33:9–10:

> As Moses went into the tent, the pillar of cloud would come down and stay at the entrance, while the LORD spoke with Moses. Whenever the people saw the pillar of cloud standing at the entrance to the tent, they all stood and worshiped, each at the entrance to his tent.

The people did not "see" God, but the cloud was a sign of his presence.

Later generations of Israelites fondly remembered the divine guidance of the two pillars: "By day you led them with a pillar of cloud, and by night with a pillar of fire to give them light on the way they were to take" (Neh. 9:12). "He spoke to them from the pillar of cloud; / they kept his statutes and the decrees he gave them" (Ps. 99:7). Christians also remembered the cloud and fire, and for many Christians the cloud became a symbol of the mysteriousness and awesomeness of God.

Leviathan, and Other Fearsome Things

Leviathans, behemoths, and dragons, oh my!

Israel today has beach resorts on the Mediterranean Sea, but in ancient times it didn't, for those fearsome pagan people known as the Philistines occupied the coast. These were sometimes known as the "Sea People," and apparently they were competent sailors and traders, as much at home on the sea as on the land.

This was never true of the Israelites, who were very much people of the land. Even though some of the kings of Israel (such as Solomon) had trading ships, most of the people of Israel did not particularly like the ocean, perhaps because they connected it with loathsome people like the Philistines.

The one book of the Old Testament that has a sea setting, Jonah, shows us that Israelites seemed to get into trouble when they went to sea. Ditto in the New Testament, where poor Paul, a prisoner on a ship bound for Rome, was shipwrecked.

If you are wondering where all this is leading, it is to the subject of sea creatures, specifically the two the book of Job mentions, *leviathan* and *behemoth*. If you have ever read Job, you know that God spoke the last chapters of the book, and he was describing to Job the many wonders of creation. Note these verses from chapter 41, a long passage describing this fearsome and mysterious creature:

> Canst thou draw out leviathan with a hook? or his tongue with a cord which thou lettest down? . . . Who can open the doors of his face? His teeth are terrible round about. His scales are his pride, shut up together as with a close seal . . . Out of his nostrils goeth smoke, as out of a seething pot or caldron . . . When he raiseth up himself, the

135

mighty are afraid . . . Upon earth there is not his like. (Job 41:1, 14–15, 20, 25, 33 KJV)

So what the heck was it? The passage indicates that the leviathan dwelled in water, so Bible translators tend to assume it referred to some actual sea beast. A whale would have fit the description, but no whale has scales. Some translators have sided with the crocodile, which was (and still is) widely feared. But no crocodile sends smoke out of its nostrils. The fact is, any attempt to match the full description in Job 41 with any real animal is bound to fail.

That leaves two possibilities. One is that the author had in mind a real creature (maybe the crocodile), but was tacking on a lot of legend and exaggeration. If you had never actually seen a crocodile, nor pictures of one, you could easily believe the frightening description in Job 41. And when you finally saw a real crocodile, you would still have to admit it was pretty darn scary.

My own opinion, and the opinion of many scholars, is that the leviathan was not a real creature at all. He was a sea monster of legend, the large, powerful, scaly, fire-breathing monster of the deep, something the land-dwelling Israelites would have had no trouble believing in. The point of Job 41 was not to provide minute details of sea life (as Jacques Cousteau would do centuries later), but to impress the reader with one idea: God the Creator made all sorts of amazing, fearsome creatures. There was no real leviathan, but the sea was full of huge and threatening creatures—the whale, the octopus, the squid, sharks, etc. The Lord God made them all.

So much for the leviathan. The book of Job also mentions the "behemoth" (40:15–24). He too was a fearsome beast, though not quite as frightening as the leviathan. He dwelled on the land as well as in the water, and Bible scholars suspect he might have been the hippopotamus or perhaps even the elephant. But as with leviathan, the details in Job don't exactly match any living beast. It is quite possible that the author of Job may have had in mind some mythical creature, a land-water beast that never existed except in people's minds.

Matters like this drive Bible translators crazy. Most have settled for the obvious thing: using the words *leviathan* and *behemoth* instead of trying to translate them. In modern versions you may find a footnote, such as one that says the leviathan was "possibly the crocodile" or another that says the behemoth was "possibly the hippopotamus."

Now, one more mythical creature, the dragon. "Praise the LORD from the earth, ye dragons, and all deeps"—so says Psalm 148:7 in the King James Version. Did the King James translators really believe in dragons, or were they simply stumped (as translators still are) by certain Hebrew words? Probably the latter. You'll find the word *dragon* many times in the King James Version, while today's versions are more accurate (probably) in using such words as "serpents" (Ps. 74:13) or even "jackals" (Job 30:29). The one place in the Bible where *dragon* really does mean *dragon* is in Revelation, where the fearsome red dragon is a symbol of the power of evil (see Rev. 12).

God strictly prohibited the people of ancient Israel to worship nature. The Ten Commandments commanded them to worship only the invisible creator God, and to make no idols. Other nations that did worship nature surrounded them, and they made idols in the shape of beasts, both real and mythical. Yet while the Israelites were not to worship the created order, they could not help but be impressed by it, as we still are today. We know a lot more about God's world than the people in ancient times did, and we feel fairly confident that leviathans, behemoths, and dragons do not exist. But this doesn't lessen the value of what the Bible says about these mythical beasts.

Job 40 and 41, with the poetic descriptions of the leviathan and behemoth, remind us that God did indeed create many amazing things. The world is still full of frightening creatures, yet the book of Job reminds us that God himself is the creator and is in control. We are not to fear or worship nature, but rather the God who made everything.

Heavenly Porter, with Attitude

—

The one gate guardian you do not mess with

Y ou no doubt connect the garden of Eden with a devil (Satan, that is, in the form of the serpent). Angels were a part of Eden, too; but not, alas, in any pleasant way. After the serpent tempted Adam and Eve, they ate the forbidden fruit, and because they disobeyed God, he banished them forever from Eden. Cherubim (angels) and a flaming sword guarded the entryway of Eden, a vivid symbol that once man had sinned, he could never go back.

A couple of things worth noting: the cherubim did not actually hold the flaming sword. It was just there, sort of floating in the air, "flashing back and forth to guard the way to the tree of life" (Gen. 3:24). We can almost picture it as something like lightning, and it was obviously a symbol of God's anger at man's disobedience.

About the cherubim: this is the Bible's first mention of them (or any type of angels), but they appear often in its pages, mostly because their gold-hewn figures adorned the top of the famous ark of the covenant. We gather that they were sort of human-shaped, but with wings instead of arms. The cherubim figures on the ark faced each other, with the tips of their wings touching (see Exod. 25:18–22). Many times the Bible speaks of God "enthroned between the cherubim."

It is hard to read Genesis 3 without feeling a touch of sadness. Man literally had it all—so long as he obeyed a simple rule about staying away from certain trees. Blame the serpent if you like, but Christians have always placed the real blame on Adam and Eve for disobeying and losing paradise for all the rest of us. The expulsion from Eden is tragic, and cherubim and the flaming sword remind us that not only was God totally serious about the expulsion but that, just as important, we can never go back.

It's Cool in the Furnace

A look at our old friends Shadrach, Meshach, and that other guy

The book of Daniel could be subtitled "The Young Men's Guide to Health, Wealth, and Happiness." The hero of the book is the young Daniel, who at a tender age found himself deported from his native country (Judah) to the capital of a conquering empire (Babylon). There a court official recruited him and three of his Jewish friends for an internship program for the Babylonian court.

The official selected interns on the basis of their physical attractiveness and intelligence. In other words, they already possessed great potential, and the royal internship program would train them for high office in this foreign land.

Daniel and his three friends passed through the program with flying colors—and they managed to surpass their peers by sticking with their own diet program. At the end of the three-year program, they became aides to the king, the mighty Nebuchadnezzar.

In another chapter in this book, we looked at Daniel's skill in interpreting dreams. This endeared him to King Nebuchadnezzar, so much so that

> he made him ruler over the entire province of Babylon and placed him in charge of all its wise men. Moreover, at Daniel's request the king appointed Shadrach, Meshach, and Abednego administrators over the province of Babylon, while Daniel himself remained at the royal court. (Dan. 2:48–49)

Does any of this sound familiar? It should, for it resembles a much earlier story in the Old Testament, the story of Joseph, Jacob's famous son, the kid with the "coat of many colors." You might recall that

Joseph's jealous brothers sold him into slavery, but instead of languishing as a slave in Egypt, he used his intelligence, eventually elevating himself (with God's help) to the post of right-hand man to the Egyptian pharaoh. The parallels to Daniel's story are amazing: moral Hebrew boy finds himself in a foreign land, shows himself wise and skilled at interpreting dreams, is promoted to being the king's trusted aide.

The Jewish boys had gone far. But the rule in life is, the higher up you are, the further the fall. They were faithful Jews, and Jews did not worship idols. Nebuchadnezzar was like many powerful people: he had a favorite idol, namely, himself. So chapter 3 of Daniel tells us that he had a huge gold statue of himself made—ninety feet high and nine feet wide. He summoned all the bigwigs in the empire to be present at the statue's dedication—and of course, they had to bow down and worship it. There was an "or else" involved: "Whoever does not fall down and worship will immediately be thrown into a blazing furnace" (v. 6).

So, with the royal orchestra providing musical accompaniment, everyone fell down and did their duty—everyone except Daniel's three friends Shadrach, Meshach, and Abednego. (Daniel himself was, happily, not present for the idolatrous scene.) Some of the court officials ratted on the three young men, happy to report that the high-ranking foreigners would experience a sudden decline in power.

The king summoned the three men and personally redelivered his ultimatum: fall down and worship the image, or be roasted. "Then what god will be able to rescue you from my hand?" (Dan. 3:15). (The king obviously did not suffer from low self-esteem. He obviously did not know much about the power of their God, either.)

The three faithful Jewish men were not terrified of the king.

> If we are thrown into the blazing furnace, the God we serve is able to save us from it, and he will rescue us from your hand, O king. But even if he does not, we want you to know, O king, that we will not serve your gods or worship the image of gold you have set up. (Dan. 3:17–18)

Wow. The three had just politely but firmly thumbed their noses at one of the mightiest men in history. The king of Babylon had the power and wealth to set up a huge gold statue and order everyone to bow down to it—everyone but these three. He was so furious he had the furnace heated seven times hotter than usual. He commanded soldiers to bind the men and throw them in—the heat was so intense that the men who did this were themselves killed.

Then, the shocker: not only were the three not killed, but they were walking around unharmed inside the furnace—along with a fourth man, who looked "like a son of the gods" (Dan. 3:25).

Nebuchadnezzar summoned the three to come out, and naturally all the Babylonian nabobs crowded around in amazement. "They saw that the fire had not harmed their bodies, nor was a hair of their heads singed; their robes were not scorched, and there was no smell of fire on them" (Dan. 3:27). God had not only saved them from death, but he saw to it that the fire had not affected them in any way. So much for tyrants and their threats of dire punishments.

Being a power-lover himself, the king was impressed by this display of divine power. He issued a royal decree: anyone who spoke a word against the God of Shadrach, Meshach, and Abednego would be cut into pieces. He then not only released the three men but gave them a promotion. In a sense, every Jew living in the empire received a promotion also, for Nebuchadnezzar had decided that the Jews' God had great power, and so no one could slander their religion without fear of punishment. The faith of the three men had benefited the faith of all their fellow believers.

An obvious question arises: who was that fourth man in the furnace, the one who looked "like a son of the gods"? The text doesn't tell us. One possible answer is that it was God himself, appearing in human form briefly. It might have been an angel. We really don't know; we know only that this figure was somehow involved in protecting the three men from the fire. One curiosity in the story is that only Nebuchadnezzar himself was able to see this mysterious figure.

This is one of the great Bible stories, a favorite for both adults and kids. The moral is clear enough: if we stay true to God and refuse to worship the world's idols, God will protect us, even in the worst circumstances. Throughout history, many persecuted people of faith have drawn strength from this story. Like all really good stories, it is timeless. Even faithful people who endure martyrdom can take heart from the story, for it is a reminder that there is a Protector who will see that his people live forever.

Blood Flood

The first of the ten plagues, and a bloody mess

You'll find many references in the Bible to "magicians," and you might wonder if these were like the magicians of today—illusionists, people who entertain by performing clever tricks of sleight of hand. They were that type of person—at times, anyway. The key difference was, their audiences were not in on the joke. That is, the biblical magicians genuinely fooled people into thinking something supernatural had occurred. This was a prescientific world, and though people weren't as stupid as you might suppose, they were probably more gullible than people today.

The great home of magic and magicians was Egypt, known to many ancients as "the land of sorcery." The pharaoh would have in his court numerous court magicians, men who could (supposedly) perform wonders. In theory these could, using "secret" rituals and lots of fancy words and phrases, make amazing things happen. Simply put, their knowing magic meant they had control over nature, or the gods, or both.

Egypt's gods were, like most pagan deities, gods of nature. The magicians, who were often priests as well, could make these gods do their bidding—or so they claimed. And one obvious way to convince people that one had such astonishing power was to perform a conjuring trick: the rabbit out of the hat, or sawing a woman in half.

Today we would applaud such a person only for performing an amazing illusion. But in ancient times the people might really believe the illusionist could work genuine magic. These people would not have made any distinction between "black" magic (used for evil purposes) and "white" magic (used for good). Any magic that did what you wanted was good.

All of this is background to Moses' entrance to the Egyptian court, where God told him to demonstrate his divine power by using his staff, which turned into a serpent on the ground. Moses had had his miraculous encounter with God at the burning bush, had seen that God could make his skin leprous and turn his staff into a serpent (Exod. 4). But he was entering the court of Pharaoh, which was swarming with magicians who could witness Moses turning his brother Aaron's staff into a snake and say, "Hey, piece of cake."

So, according to Exodus 7:12, Pharaoh's magicians could also perform the staff-into-serpent trick. "Each one threw down his staff and it became a snake." This may have been momentarily embarrassing for Moses. The feat God did now seemed commonplace. These court flunkies were just as powerful as his God. Or were they? "But Aaron's staff swallowed up their staffs." Hmm. So much for Egyptian magic. It had power, true, but God was still more powerful.

Naturally we have to pause and ask: if God truly did turn Aaron's staff into a snake, how did the magicians mimic the trick? We don't know—though certainly not through the power of God. Magicians in the Middle East long ago perfected the trick of pressing a snake's neck in such a way that it grew rigid like a stick—and could be released later on. Perhaps the magicians' "staffs" were really rigid snakes turning into writhing snakes. The only explanation for Aaron's snake devouring the others is, simply, the power of God.

One other explanation would have been obvious to an earlier generation, though not to us: perhaps the magicians had tapped into the power of demons. Sounds far-fetched, but do not rule it out. It would not be the last time in history people had done frightening things using black magic.

But alas, the serpent trick did not impress the one important person present: "Yet Pharaoh's heart became hard and he would not listen to them, just as the LORD had said" (Exod. 7:13). Obviously it would take something more dramatic to change the king's mind.

And that brings us to the ten plagues of Egypt. All were so dramatic, and so bizarre, that we could easily devote a single chapter to each in this book. We will cover only two, the first and the last, though we will give the others a quickie treatment. Much of what is true about the first was true of the others as well.

The plagues were all a bold, harsh slap at nature religion. We already stated that the Egyptians worshiped nature gods. Their many gods were depicted with human bodies and the heads of familiar animals—the jackal, the hawk, the crocodile. The crown the pharaoh wore had figures of a vulture and a cobra on it—repulsive creatures, but both symbols of the power of nature.

Israel's God was not a god of nature—he was God *over* nature, as the plagues proved. He was bigger than the Egyptian gods. He was bigger than the pharaoh, who was himself supposed to be divine. And like most men of great power, he probably believed he was.

Now, to the first plague. The next morning Moses and Aaron went down to the river—*the* river, that is, the mighty Nile (even though the original Hebrew Bible never names it). Pharaoh was there, not just admiring the view but probably attending an annual ceremony in which he officially "greeted" the river's annual flood. You might already know that Egypt is practically a rainless country, and that its crops and its very life depended on this annual (and predictable) flooding of the Nile River (which occurred, by the way, roughly from June to September). The ancient Greek author Herodotus noted that "all Egypt is the gift of the Nile," and he was right.

In fact, years after the events recorded in Exodus, Egyptians referred to Israel as the "land that depends on rain"—and they meant it as an insult. In the Egyptians' view, the river was a god, a divine force that blessed them with the water needed for irrigating their crops. But that god was in for a showdown with the real God.

In the sight of Pharaoh, Moses struck the river waters with his staff, and the waters "changed into blood" (Exod. 7:20). The fish in the river died, and we all know how vile rotted fish smell. The water became so loathsome that the people could not drink it.

Now, we have to tread softly when interpreting this. One option is to take it all literally and conclude that the river water did indeed turn into blood, which really would smell and would kill the fish also. But there is a natural explanation that many people of faith are willing to accept: the waters turned bloodred, due to red earth deposits that sometimes flow down in the annual flood, along with some microorganisms that poison the fish. (Your author lives near the Gulf of Mexico, which is prone to "red tide," a microorganism that causes fish to die and rot on the beaches.)

Ancient Egyptian writers at different periods lamented that the river had "become blood," and they described conditions similar to what Exodus describes. This is a natural explanation for what occurred, but it does not take away from the power of God at all, for it was surely God who timed it in this way. Curiously, Exodus tells us that the court magicians duplicated the miracle "by their secret arts" (Exod. 7:22). How they did this is a mystery.

Though this "blood flood" probably had natural causes, it was rare enough that most of the Egyptians had probably never seen one, so it made an impact—but not on Pharaoh. So there followed the other plagues. The land swarmed with frogs, which no doubt had a connection with the "Red Nile" plague. Then came gnats (which might better be translated "mosquitoes"—annoying critters, either ones), also related to the river. Then came flies, which would relate to the rotting fish and frogs.

These first four were dramatic, of course, but mostly just annoying. All four left Pharaoh unmoved, so the plagues became more intense. The fifth was a pestilence on livestock—again, another slap at nature. The sixth was boils—not just on beasts but on people as well. The seventh was hail, which is very rare in Egypt, making the hailstorm all that more dramatic. Hail cannot only damage crops in the field but can be downright dangerous, even killing cattle in the field. Imagine the effect on the Egyptians: their ever-sunny sky (the sun was a god, of course) was not smiling on them—instead, the sky was dropping hailstones, ruining their crops and harming their stock.

The eighth plague showed nature at its worst: locusts, the devastating grasshoppers that arrive in huge swarms and devour every plant in sight. Then the ninth plague: darkness, perhaps caused by the powerful desert wind known as the *khamsin*, which blows in so fiercely, bringing dust and sand, that it can block out the sun for days at a time. The tenth and final plague was the deaths of the Egyptians' firstborn sons.

Several of the plagues were natural, meaning they were phenomena that did and do occur in Egypt now and then. Again, the timing was important: God knew when the plagues were coming and passed his word on to Moses, so that they seemed to happen at Moses' bidding. The

Egyptians had witnessed locusts before, as well as gnats, flies, perhaps hail and darkness as well. Yet collectively, they pointed out something: Moses' God seemed to be in control of all these things, and the Egyptians' nature gods seemed powerless.

The account of the plagues is more than a vital piece of history. Yes, it is important for us to know that God used his power over creation to persuade the pharaoh (finally!) to free the Israelites from slavery. It is important for us to know that he did, and does, watch out for his people.

But the other important lesson is this: the world's so-called "gods" are not gods at all. The gods of Egypt with their jackal heads, falcon heads, cat heads, and so on, were mere pieces of stone. The real God was and is invisible—and more powerful than all the false gods together.

Lying and Dying

Till death did them part

In the popular children's story, the wooden puppet Pinocchio's punishment for lying was having his nose grow long. The book of Acts tells a frightening story about a married couple who received a much more dramatic punishment for their dishonesty.

This happened among the first Christians in Jerusalem, a loving fellowship of people that had responded to the apostles' preaching about Jesus Christ.

> All the believers were one in heart and mind. No one claimed that any of his possessions was his own, but they shared everything they had. With great power the apostles continued to testify to the resurrection of the Lord Jesus, and much grace was upon them all. There were no needy persons among them. For from time to time those who owned lands or houses sold them, brought the money from the sales and put it at the apostles' feet, and it was distributed to anyone as he had need. (Acts 4:32–35)

Sounds wonderful, doesn't it? A community of faith, a fellowship of people who honored Christ as Lord and Savior, and who genuinely treated each other as brothers and sisters. While they had their minds fixed on heaven, they didn't neglect each other's worldly needs, and so "there were no needy persons among them," for those with money and possessions chipped in to aid those who had little. It was a sort of "Christian communism," and it seemed to be working beautifully.

But the book of Acts is very honest about history, and it shows the early Christians warts and all. True, there were a lot of love and a lot of

147

sharing. But these Christians were still human beings, still subject to self-ishness and greed and dishonesty.

Acts mentions one particular Christian who sold some of his land and gave the money to the fellowship. This was a certain Joseph, who was given the nickname Barnabas (called the "Son of Encouragement" in Acts 4:36), and he would play a major role in the spread of the gospel, for he would become a missionary partner of the great apostle Paul.

But immediately after Acts praises the generosity of Barnabas, it presents us with Exhibit B, a married couple who did what Barnabas did . . . but with a slight difference.

> Now a man named Ananias, together with his wife Sapphira, also sold a piece of property. With his wife's full knowledge he kept back part of the money for himself, but brought the rest and put it at the apostles' feet.
>
> Then Peter said, "Ananias, how is it that Satan has so filled your heart that you have lied to the Holy Spirit and have kept for yourself some of the money you received for the land? Didn't it belong to you before it was sold? And after it was sold, wasn't the money at your disposal? What made you think of doing such a thing? You have not lied to men but to God." (Acts 5:1–4)

Now, here is the dramatic sting in this bizarre story: "When Ananias heard this, he fell down and died. And great fear seized all who heard what had happened. Then the young men came forward, wrapped up his body, and carried him out and buried him" (Acts 5:5).

If you react with horror to this, you would not be the first reader to do so. But read on:

> About three hours later his wife came in, not knowing what had happened. Peter asked her, "Tell me, is this the price you and Ananias got for the land?"
>
> "Yes," she said, "that is the price."
>
> Peter said to her, "How could you agree to test the Spirit of the Lord? Look! The feet of the men who buried your husband are at the door, and they will carry you out also."
>
> At that moment she fell down at his feet and died. Then the young men came in and, finding her dead, carried her out and buried her be-

side her husband. Great fear seized the whole church and all who heard about these events. (Acts 5:7–11)

Sounds pretty gruesome, doesn't it? Chapter 4 of Acts paints this rosy picture of the loving fellowship of Christians, and suddenly in chapter 5, two of those people dropped dead because they told the apostles a lie. Peter and the apostles come across as extremely cruel, and death certainly seems like a harsh punishment for telling one simple lie.

Keep some things in mind, though: Acts does not attribute the death of Ananias or Sapphira to the apostles, nor to the power of God. Peter did not pronounce any kind of curse on the couple; he simply let them know that he was aware that they had lied about the amount of money they got for the property they sold. Frankly, Acts does not give us a clue about what brought about the death. In the case of Sapphira, the shock of learning of her husband's death could have been a factor in her own.

What was the real offense here? As Peter pointed out, no one required the couple to sell their property, or to pass all the proceeds on to the Christian fellowship. They chose to do so, and they chose to keep some of the money for themselves—so far, so good. But they also chose to lie about it. In other words, they wanted the Christians to think they were more generous than they actually were.

It doesn't sound like a huge sin to us, but their deception introduced hypocrisy into the fellowship, and the newly begun Christian movement had no place for it. It needed people whose motives and words were pure and trustworthy—people like the faithful Barnabas, not a married couple who would conspire to lie about what they did.

Perhaps the main reason Acts includes this unsettling story appears in the last sentence: "Great fear seized the whole church and all who heard about these events." And rightly so. The newborn fellowship was for people who feared God, people who were willing to deal honestly with each other. The deaths of Ananias and Sapphira, though they offend our modern sensibilities, sent a message to any people who thought of converting to the faith: join our fellowship only if you can be totally forthright. There is no place here for lying and hypocrisy.

Goaded to War

―

One of those one-paragraph heroes of Judges

The book of Judges would be more appropriately called the "book of Heroes" or "book of Military Deliverers," as I've noted elsewhere in this book. The "judges" were not somber men in black robes, but men of action, men of war. They were "judges" only in the sense that they brought justice, that is, they delivered the Israelites from their oppressors.

The Bible tells some of the judges' stories in great detail, notably those of Samson, Gideon, and Jephthah. A few are barely more than names, though they are remembered for doing God's will by fighting off Israel's enemies.

One of these one-paragraph wonders is Shamgar, which Judges 3:31 mentions as "Shamgar, son of Anath, who struck down six hundred Philistines with an oxgoad. He too saved Israel." The biblical account mentions several of the other judges as "judging" Israel for a certain number of years. Shamgar isn't, so perhaps his oxgoad incident was a one-time action. It certainly impressed the Israelites—and no doubt the Philistines as well.

We use the word *goad* all the time in its figurative sense—to goad is to provoke, urge, nudge. That is exactly what a literal goad does: nudges along cattle or other livestock. It was a wooden shaft with a pointed tip, something like a spear. How exactly Shamgar employed it in war the Bible does not tell us, but apparently he was good at it, whatever his method was. Like the judge Samson, who used the jawbone of a donkey to slay the Philistines, Shamgar proved that the Israelites didn't have to rely on the usual weapons of war to get at their enemies.

In fact, that may be the whole point of the Shamgar passage: the

150

Philistines were notable for their skill in ironworking, meaning that their weapons were more technologically advanced than those of the Israelites. But the Israelites not only had God on their side, they could improvise skillfully when it came to weapons. Technology is an amazing and powerful force to have on one's side, but God is a greater aid.

Making a Fire in the Desert

Moses and his shoeless encounter

If someone asks you who the main character in the Old Testament is, the obvious answer is "God." But certainly the most important *human* character is the great man Moses, the liberator and the lawgiver. No wonder the man became the centerpiece of some unforgettable movies—not only the classic *The Ten Commandments* with Charlton Heston, but many others, including a very popular animated film of recent years, *The Prince of Egypt*. In our secular age, when a major Hollywood company can make a profitable movie about a character from the Bible, you know that character must have been an amazing man with a colorful and dramatic life.

Recall that, if things had gone according to human plan, Moses would have had no life at all. The Egyptian pharaoh, fearing that the Hebrew slaves were too numerous, ordered all the male infants killed. The baby Moses was saved because his mother floated him in the river in a basket while his sister watched over him. None other than Pharaoh's daughter found the waterborne infant, and she raised him in her own home. An interesting twist: the slave child, destined to be destroyed by royal decree, grew up at the royal court.

Then another plot twist: the adult Moses witnessed the harsh labor of his fellow Hebrews. He saw an Egyptian slave driver beating one of the slaves. He killed the Egyptian and hid him in the sand. Pharaoh learned of the deed, and once again he threatened Moses' life. Moses fled, far away to Midian, where a shepherd who had seven daughters took him in. Naturally Moses married one of the girls.

Moses the Hebrew, Moses the adopted Egyptian, and then Moses the adopted Midianite: for all he knew, he would end his days herding flocks in Midian. But God had other plans. The old pharaoh died, but the new one continued the oppression of the slaves, and God was not pleased. Who could have guessed that the shepherd in Midian would be God's instrument of liberation?

"Now Moses was tending the flock of Jethro his father-in-law, the priest of Midian, and he led the flock to the far side of the desert and came to Horeb, the mountain of God" (Exod. 3:1). Thus begins in earnest the story of the liberator. Note that Moses was at "Horeb, the mountain of God." Horeb is another name for Sinai, the same mountain where, years later, Moses would receive the Ten Commandments from God.

But for now: "There the angel of the LORD appeared to him in flames of fire from within a bush. Moses saw that though the bush was on fire it did not burn up. So Moses thought, 'I will go over and see this strange sight—why the bush does not burn up'" (Exod. 3:2–3).

Don't be put off by the phrase "angel of the Lord." No, that did not mean that a white-robed, winged being was in the bush. An angel could sometimes be invisible—an "angel of the LORD" was sometimes a round-about way of saying "the Lord himself." What was more important here was that God himself called to Moses from the bush.

Then he ordered Moses, "Take off your sandals, for the place where you are standing is holy ground" (Exod. 3:5). There was nothing sacred about the soil itself, of course. It was "holy" because at that moment God was there.

Then, some of the most famous words in the whole Bible: "I am the God of your father, the God of Abraham, the God of Isaac, and the God of Jacob" (Exod. 3:6). A pretty intimidating encounter, and the now shoeless Moses was afraid to look at God, so he hid his face.

Pause for a moment and consider the bush. Was there some natural explanation for it? Some authorities say that certain types of desert shrub can ignite in the heat, and can burn for a while without being consumed. Perhaps so, and perhaps that is what got Moses' attention at first. But the only explanation for God's voice is—well, God's voice. And by the way, the Bible uses fire often as a symbol of God's presence.

Back to Moses: God then told him that he had seen the misery of the Hebrews in Egypt and intended to bring them to Canaan, "a land flowing with milk and honey." And he would send Moses to Pharaoh as liberator. Moses, now only a humble shepherd, asked the obvious question:

"Who am I, that I should go to Pharaoh?" And God gave the obvious reply: "I will be with you" (Exod. 3:8, 11–12).

Comforting words, but Moses was still perplexed. What, he asked God, would he tell them was God's name? God's reply: "I AM WHO I AM" (Exod. 3:14). In other words, no name at all, just an affirmation: "I AM." All the other "gods," the false gods of the pagans, have names. But Israel's is so amazing that he can't be captured in a mere name.

After all the thousands of pages and tons of ink that have been spent on interpreting this passage in the Bible, this is what it all comes down to: the true God has no name, no "tag," no "handle." Humans have names, and the false gods have names, but the true God is too big for a name. He just *is*.

God then explained to Moses how he was to go to the leaders of Israel and tell them of the divine plan to free them from Egypt. Moses feared they would be skeptical. He had seen God and heard his voice, but what if the others didn't believe him?

So God gave him a sign: he told Moses to throw his staff on the ground, and it turned into a snake. Moses was frightened. (Who wouldn't be?) But God told him to reach out for its tail, and it became a staff again. Then, another sign. God told Moses to put his hand inside his cloak. He did, then drew it out again. His skin was white as snow. Then God restored it.

Any rational explanation for these events? None at all. You might guess that Moses was having hallucinations in the heat of the desert, but if you believe that, then the whole basis of the Jewish religion (and later, Christianity) was some shepherd's delusion. In the ordinary course of things, bushes do not burn without eventually being consumed, the voice of God does not come from a desert shrub, a wooden staff does not turn into a snake, and a man's hand does not suddenly turn white and then become normal again. The key word is *ordinary*.

But something big was in the works here: the liberation of a huge group of slaves, their journey to their homeland in Canaan, the giving of God's law to them—and through them, to the whole human race. This was a major project, and we should not be surprised that some miracles happened along the way. The burning bush was the first of many, and over the centuries both Jews and Christians have used the burning bush as a symbol of God's presence. It is an appropriate one, a reminder that God is with his people, sometimes in dramatic ways.

The Knock-Kneed King of Persia

The very first handwriting on the wall

You hear it all the time, the phrase "the handwriting on the wall," meaning something like an omen of one's fate (usually unpleasant). How many people know that the phrase comes from the Bible—specifically, from the book of Daniel, where it is one of the most colorful and bizarre stories in a very colorful and bizarre book.

The story takes place at a feast given by a Babylonian king named Belshazzar. That name *Belshazzar* used to give Bible scholars fits, because for a long time the archaeologists couldn't find any evidence that such a person existed. In other words, there was a feeling that his story in Daniel 5 was pure fiction. But the archaeologists finally dug up some clay tablets that confirmed that, yes, there was a real Belshazzar, and he was the son of the last king of Babylon, Nabonidus.

Daniel 5 says Belshazzar was a king, and we gather that he was serving in that role when his father was absent. (The title *regent* would have applied.) The passage also says the famous king Nebuchadnezzar was the "father" of Belshazzar (v. 2), but the Bible sometimes used "father" in the broader sense of "ancestor."

Belshazzar, at the head of a mighty empire, had no idea his life and his kingdom were about to end. He had thrown a lavish party, inviting a thousand nobles, with the wine flowing freely. The powerful love to show off, and during this banquet, Belshazzar had his servants bring in some items that would have been very important to the Jewish readers of Daniel: the gold utensils that the Babylonians had taken from the temple in Jerusalem.

Belshazzar was showing off some of the war booty that his granddad Nebuchadnezzar had stolen. Not only did he show them off, but his guests, wives, and concubines drank from them. Daniel's Jewish readers would have felt their blood pressure rising as they read this: a heathen king was having his heathen guests drink from utensils that were made to be used in the house of God.

And to make matters worse, "as they drank the wine, they praised the gods of gold and silver, of bronze, iron, wood and stone" (Dan. 5:4). In short, they were defiling the cups taken from God's temple while at the same time praising their own idols. Surely the God of Israel was watching this and was not pleased.

And surely enough, he was not.

> Suddenly the fingers of a human hand appeared and wrote on the plaster of the wall, near the lampstand in the royal palace. The king watched the hand as it wrote. His face turned pale and he was so frightened that his knees knocked together and his legs gave way. (Dan. 5:5–6)

A lovely touch: the mighty ruler of Babylon, presiding over a lavish banquet, suddenly turned into a mass of quivering jelly.

What did the hand write? Words that no one in the room could understand. So the terrified king sent for his court magicians. He promised them purple robes, gold chains, and high office if they could interpret what this mysterious hand wrote on the wall. None of them could.

The queen offered a suggestion: she knew of a wise man, one with "insight and intelligence and wisdom like that of the gods," a man that the great Nebuchadnezzar had promoted to high office. The man was the Jewish fellow Daniel, who could "interpret dreams, explain riddles, and solve difficult problems" (Dan. 5:11–12).

So the puzzled, frightened king sent for Daniel. "I have heard that the spirit of the gods is in you and that you have insight, intelligence, and outstanding wisdom" (Dan. 5:14). The king repeated his promise: a purple robe, a gold chain, third highest rank in the whole kingdom.

Daniel's reply is a classic: "You may keep your gifts for yourself and give your rewards to someone else. Nevertheless, I will read the writing for the king, and tell him what it means" (Dan. 5:17). Before he did so, however, Daniel paused for a brief sermonette: he reminded Belshazzar that his relative, the mighty Nebuchadnezzar, had been proud and haughty—and had been struck down into madness until he humbled himself before God.

But Belshazzar had not humbled himself. "Instead, you have set yourself up as the Lord of heaven. You had the goblets from his temple brought to you . . . You did not honor the God who holds in his hand your life and all your ways. Therefore he sent the hand that wrote the inscription" (Dan. 5:23–24).

You get the definite impression that Daniel already knew what the hand had written even before he saw it. Perhaps that was why he declined the king's gifts. He knew he would never make use of them.

The words written on the wall were "*Mene, Mene, Tekel, Parsin*"— translated, "numbered, numbered, weighed, divided." Daniel interpreted it this way: Belshazzar's days were numbered; God weighed him on the scales and found him lacking; God would divide his kingdom and give it to others.

Not exactly the message Belshazzar wanted to hear, of course, but he did make good on his promise, and Daniel received a purple robe and gold chain, and made third man in the kingdom.

Daniel did not give the king a timetable for these unpleasant predictions, so perhaps Belshazzar shrugged the whole thing off and figured it would never happen, or would happen in the distant future. But things moved swiftly: "That very night Belshazzar, king of the Babylonians, was slain, and Darius the Mede took over the kingdom" (Dan. 5:30–31).

Darius the Mede headed the Persian empire. The Persians captured Babylon in October of 539 B.C. The Greek historian Herodotus claimed that they took Babylon by surprise as the royals sat at a feast. You might not accept the story of the disembodied hand writing on the wall, but the rest of the story is on very firm historical ground.

The point of the story is not the hand, of course, but the pride of Belshazzar. Like his more famous grandfather, he let haughtiness bring him down. Nebuchadnezzar had sacked Jerusalem, burned the temple, and made off with its valuables. Belshazzar had mocked the temple utensils by using them as drinking vessels for his boozy friends. Proud individuals fall, as Belshazzar did, and proud empires fall, as Babylon did. In time the Persian empire that had conquered Babylon would fall, too.

The Old Testament's Teetotaling Hippies

Those longhaired, nondrinking Nazirites

Remember Samson, the Hebrew strongman with the long hair—and ill-fated infatuation with Delilah? One of the things we often forget about Samson is that he belonged to a religious group known as the Nazirites, and long hair was one of the trademarks of the group.

The name *Nazirite* has nothing to do with Nazareth, Jesus' hometown. The name comes from the Hebrew *nazir*, meaning "vow," and the Nazirites were "people of the vow." They were individuals who took vows not to touch wine, not to cut their hair (including their beards), and not to touch a dead body. Numbers 6 describes the Nazirite rules in detail.

A person could choose to be a Nazirite for a certain period (minimum of one month), or a whole lifetime. If he took vows for a certain period, at the end of that period the person would cut his hair and offer it up to God by burning it on the altar. Whatever the time frame he chose, he took the vows very seriously. Though the Nazirites' vows made them "separate to the Lord," they did not live apart from the other Israelites but among them.

The Bible frankly does not explain the significance of the three vows. We can assume that renouncing alcohol was a symbol of renouncing all sensual pleasures. The other two—letting the hair grow, and avoiding contact with a dead body—are not so easily explained. We do know that many ancient peoples had the habit of letting their hair grow during some period when they were seeking divine help, then afterward dedicating the cut hair to their god.

In most cultures, hair was (and is) a sign of strength, something that became abundantly clear in the case of Samson, whose superhuman strength vanished after his famous haircut. (And to show that some things never change, have you noticed the booming business in hair transplants and other hair-loss treatments today? Most men do *not* want to be bald.)

Three of the Nazirites became famous. Samson I have already mentioned. Another was Samuel, the judge who crowned Israel's first two kings. And perhaps most famous of all was John the Baptist, Jesus' kinsman. All three of these had taken the Nazirite vows for a lifetime—or more accurately, their parents had taken the vows, for all three were dedicated to the Lord before their births.

In each case, a woman who had been childless suddenly learned that God had taken pity on her and was allowing her to conceive. And in each case she showed her gratitude to the Lord by dedicating the child to him as a Nazirite.

Historians tell us that Nazirites (the temporary, not the permanent kind) were fairly common in Israel at certain periods, including the New Testament period. In fact, it appears that the apostle Paul may have taken the vows for a while, as we see in Acts 18:18: "Before he sailed, he had his hair cut off at Cenchrea because of a vow he had taken." Acts 21:24 mentions four men who "made a vow" and were about to have their heads sheared, so we can assume these were temporary Nazirites.

In our contemporary culture we find it hard to believe anyone would deliberately choose to renounce anything for a religious reason, so the Nazirite vows might seem merely silly. And a Christian might raise the obvious question: in what way do the vows really make a person spiritually better? A person could take the Nazirite vows for a lifetime and still be a despicable human being.

But the fact that the apostle Paul and some other Christians took the vows ought to make us ask if they had some value after all. Perhaps the vows, and the lifestyle changes they entailed, served as reminders of the main point of it all: that the person was consecrated, dedicated to the Lord, and in some sense separated from the larger world. That is a valid goal for all of us.

Righteous Noah—Well, Usually

The ark fellow—drunk, undressed, and cursing

You must remember Noah—the one righteous man on earth when everyone else was wicked. Noah pleased God, which is why God chose him (along with his wife, three sons, and three daughters-in-law) to survive the great Flood and repopulate the earth.

It's a wonderful story, and Noah is one of the most admirable characters in the Bible. But in Genesis 9 we see a different side of the saintly man. After his family left the ark, Noah began farming and planted a vineyard. Then he got drunk "and lay uncovered inside his tent" (v. 21).

Ham, one of his three sons, saw Noah naked and told his two brothers, Shem and Japheth. Those two apparently did not wish to see their father naked, so they took a garment and walked backward toward Noah, covering him with it without ever looking at him.

Noah awoke, realized what had happened, and placed a blessing on Shem and Japheth. He placed a curse on . . . not Ham, but on Ham's son Canaan, who, Noah decreed, would be "the lowest of slaves" to Shem and Japheth (Gen. 9:25). Why not curse Ham himself? We'll return to that shortly. For now, let's look at the parts that make perfect sense.

Noah was a good man—one who on this occasion happened to get drunk. The Bible never mentions wine or drinking before this, so some people credit Noah with inventing wine. The Bible doesn't say so. It says only he was drunk and lay uncovered (or "naked" in some translations), meaning he was making a fool of himself.

The sons Shem and Japheth did what good sons would do: show some respect by covering up Dad and not giggling or mocking him because of the embarrassing situation. Ham, we gather, found it kind of amusing: old Dad was drunk and naked there in the tent. He wasn't exactly honoring his father.

That explains the blessing on Shem and Japheth. But why did Noah curse Canaan, Ham's son, instead of Ham himself? Genesis 9 has already made the point more than once that "Ham was the father of Canaan" (vv. 18, 22). Every Israelite who read Genesis 9 knew who Canaan was—the ancestor of the wicked, idol-worshiping Canaanites, the people whose land God gave to the Israelites. So this story is a kind of explanation of why the Canaanites were so bad: they came from "bad stock," the disrespectful Ham. Though Ham had other sons that the Bible names, Noah cursed only Canaan. We really don't know why.

One thing worth noting: the Bible took nakedness and also parental respect very seriously. Ham's sin—seeing his father naked—sounds like no sin at all to us, but the Israelites would not have laughed it off. Parents in those days were not "buddies" to their children. There was more formality in the parent-child relationship, and kids were expected to know that and accept it.

A father was to be treated with dignity—even when, as on this occasion, he wasn't acting very dignified himself. Shem and Japheth understood that even when Dad wasn't at his best, a good son would still treat him with profound respect.

Great Special Effects—
Ancient Israel Style

Elijah's close encounter, with a fabulous ending

Earth, Wind & Fire was the name of a popular music group, but long before that it was a good description of the prophet Elijah's very close encounter with God.

Elijah lived during the reign of one of Israel's nastier kings, the idol-worshiping, immoral Ahab, who was married to the equally immoral Jezebel, fanatically devoted to the false god Baal. Elsewhere in this book we look at the famous contest between Elijah and the Baal prophets, which 1 Kings 18 relates. Following that fateful encounter, Jezebel was not pleased at having her Baal prophets killed, so she swore she would have Elijah slain, and soon.

The contest with the Baal prophets had been a victory for both God and Elijah. It was an "up" moment, but following it was one of the most "down" moments in Elijah's life. On the run from Jezebel, he hid out in the desert. Sitting under a tree, he prayed to God to take his life. (Consider the irony: he fled from Jezebel's threat on his life, then prayed for God to end his life. But it made sense: better to die at God's hand than at Jezebel's.)

God had no intention of taking the life of one his finest servants. Elijah fell asleep, and when he awoke he found food and water at hand—provided by an angel. Feeling refreshed and vigorous, he set out for Horeb—another name for Sinai. It was the "mountain of God" (1 Kings 19:8), and on it Elijah found a cave and spent the night.

There God spoke to him, asking him why he was there. Elijah poured out his grief: he was the only one left in Israel who truly served God, and Israel's rulers were trying to kill him. He was on the very mountain where Moses had received God's holy commandments—and the people of Israel had failed to live by them.

Then followed the "special effects": God ordered him to pay attention, "for the LORD is about to pass by." First, a mighty wind blew through, shattering the rocks—"but the LORD was not in the wind." Then, an earthquake—"but the LORD was not in the earthquake." Then a fire—"but the LORD was not in the fire" (1 Kings 19:11–12).

After all that drama "came a gentle whisper" (1 Kings 19:12). Frankly, the words of the old King James Version are even better: "a still small voice." Elijah went and stood at the opening to the cave. God spoke to him again, this time with some orders: there are over seven thousand faithful people still in Israel, people who have not fallen into Baal worship. (In other words: *Stop feeling sorry for yourself, Elijah, for you are not alone.*) Go and anoint a new king of Israel, one who will stamp out Baal worship. And go and anoint a new prophet to succeed you.

God understood something basic about human nature: the best thing for a depressed person to do is to get moving—instead of wallowing in self-pity and despair, *do something*.

This was the second time a man of God had "seen" God on the mountain called Horeb, or Sinai. Moses had beheld the glory of God passing by (Exod. 33), and now Elijah had.

First Kings 19 makes it clear that God was not "in" the wind, earthquake, or fire, but in the "gentle whisper." There are different ways to interpret this, but the probable meaning is that God was not just a force of nature (which Elijah already knew) but could work things in a quiet way.

Elijah, the bold and fiery prophet, needed to be reminded that God sometimes worked in dramatic ways, but not always. He could sometimes be God of the spectacular, the awesome, special-effects God—but sometimes he was the "still small voice."

Heads Are Gonna Roll

—

A temple, and a lovely place for mass murder

Israel had some truly vile kings, but none had a worse reputation than Ahab. Led by his wife, Ahab gave his enthusiastic support to the cult of the false god Baal. His descendants did the same, and God decided to stamp out Ahab's dynasty. The man who did the job was one of Ahab's officials, Jehu.

We look at Jehu's treatment of Ahab's son Ahaziah and wife, Jezebel, in another chapter. There were still plenty of members of Ahab's clan remaining, so Jehu had lots of work to do.

According to 2 Kings 10:1, there were "seventy sons of the house of Ahab." It might be that "sons" means "descendants," so it would also include grandsons. But it is quite possible that Ahab did have seventy sons, considering that the king probably had several wives and concubines. Whatever the relationship to Ahab was, Jehu had no intention of letting them survive. Evil is not genetically inherited, but apparently all of Ahab's descendants were proving just as vile as the old man had been, and God wanted the whole clan destroyed.

So Jehu sent a message to the royal officials: cut off the heads of the princes. The officials had heard that Jehu had already killed the king of Israel, the king of Judah, and Jezebel as well, and he seemed to have the army (and God) on his side. So the royal officials put up no resistance. They did as Jehu requested, and they sent him a gift: the heads of the seventy princes—in baskets. Jehu gave his servant an order: "Put them in two piles at the entrance of the city gate" (2 Kings 10:8).

Why there? So everyone would see them, of course. Jehu was making a point: *Ahab's family was out, and I'm in.* He proceeded to kill any of Ahab's friends or supporters. "He destroyed them, according to the word of the LORD spoken to Elijah" (2 Kings 10:17).

A lot of blood had been shed, but it wasn't over. The real point of Jehu's crusade was not stamping out Ahab's family, but stamping out the Baal cult. He hadn't advertised that fact, so he employed a clever ruse: he announced to the people that he, too, was a Baal-worshiper—even more devoted than Ahab had been. He ordered everyone in Samaria, the capital city, to gather for a great worship service for Baal. He sent word throughout Israel for all the Baal priests to be present. And secretly, he made sure that no ministers of the true God were present.

Jehu posted eighty men to guard the temple entrances. He went through the motions of making sacrifices to Baal, then ordered the guards: "Go in and kill them; let no one escape." They not only killed all the Baal priests and the many worshipers, but tore down the temple entirely. The account ends with this poetic finish: "and people have used it for a latrine to this day" (2 Kings 10:25, 27).

Jehu did not prove to be an ideal king, but God did reward him for stamping out Baal worship. Jehu and his descendants ruled for another three generations.

A seriously bloody story, yes? Seventy princes beheaded, their heads piled up at the city gates. A temple full of people butchered. It all strikes us as pretty barbaric, even if the goal (getting rid of a false religion) was admirable. Certainly no Christian today would approve of murdering the followers of other religions.

But the story is a reminder of how a past age looked at worship and morality: *they mattered*. The Old Testament authors firmly believed that religion was not just a matter of personal taste. There was one true God, Israel's God, and the other gods were false, and following those gods involved idol worship and low moral standards as well. No one would suggest that we try to duplicate what Jehu did, but perhaps we ought to take our own religion and morals a little more seriously.

The Old Testament Trinity

Three visitors, or one—or three in one?

Centuries ago Christians agreed that the one God is also a trinity—meaning the Father, the Son, and the Holy Spirit. In some mysterious way these three exist as one—three in one, and one in three. One God—but three "Persons" (and our human vocabulary isn't really adequate to explain this).

We base the belief in the Trinity on the New Testament with its numerous references to the Father, Son, and Spirit. But Christians also believe the Trinity existed long before the New Testament—before the world existed, in fact. So Bible readers have wondered if the Old Testament gives any previews of the Trinity.

At the very beginning, in Genesis 1:26, God said, "Let us make man in our image, in our likeness." Note the plural pronouns—"us" and "our." Who was "us"? Some interpreters say God was speaking to his angels—the heavenly court. Others say the "us" was the Trinity. We can't be sure.

Consider another passage in Genesis: in chapter 18, we learn that "the LORD" appeared in the form of three men to the patriarch Abraham. Being a good and hospitable man, Abraham entertained the three "men" graciously (not knowing he was entertaining the Lord, of course). The passage says that "the LORD" (which of the three men was speaking?) predicted that when he came by at a later time, Abraham's elderly wife, Sarah, would have a child.

This passage fascinates and frustrates Bible readers. It refers to "the LORD" and "he"—but also insists that three men, not just one, visited Abraham. Who were the three? God and two angels in human form? Some readers have assumed that the three visitors were the Trinity; that Abraham didn't know it, but visiting him were the Father, Son, and Holy

Spirit. Many Christians, especially in the Eastern Orthodox churches, are fascinated by this story of the "Old Testament Trinity," and there are many paintings showing the Trinity at Abraham's table.

There is something to be said for the theory that the three visitors were God and two angels, because Genesis 18:16–22 tells us that the three began walking toward Sodom. Two continued on toward Sodom, "but Abraham remained standing before the LORD." Later, in 19:1, we learn that "the two angels arrived at Sodom in the evening."

God somehow appeared to Abraham in human form, which tells us we ought always to be on our best behavior. How do we know the person we encounter in our daily lives is not God himself, or an angel?

Yep, That Old Lions' Den Story

Old stuff, true, but solid gold anyway

If you ever attended Sunday school, you surely must have studied that great story from the Old Testament: the good man Daniel was thrown into a den with lions—and his God miraculously protected him. Like all good stories that kids love, it has a lot in it for adults, too.

Young Daniel had an amazing ability to survive and thrive in some truly unpromising situations. His family was among the many Jewish folk deported to Babylonia when that mighty empire conquered the little kingdom of Judah. But Daniel, attractive and intelligent, was among the Jewish lads chosen to serve as interns at the Babylonian court.

Daniel served well in the pagan court while managing to hold on to his own moral standards. He lived through the reign of the mighty King Nebuchadnezzar, who went insane, and he endured the fall of the last Babylonian king, the luckless Belshazzar (of the "handwriting on the wall" fame). Kings had come and gone, and so had one of the great empires of the world (Babylon), but Daniel and his God endured.

In chapter 6 of the book of Daniel, the man in power was Darius the Mede, head of the sprawling Persian empire. Daniel, the Jewish man who had held high office under the Babylonians, was made one of Darius's officials as well. Daniel was probably optimistic, because the Persians were notoriously more tolerant about religion than the Babylonians had been. That is, they were pretty willing to let the people they conquered practice their own religions. Daniel was about to find out whether the Persians were as tolerant as he had heard.

Extremely bright, competent people go far in this world—and they also arouse a lot of jealousy. Daniel was a jewel among Darius's offi-

168

cials, so many of the others were devoured with envy—partly because he was a foreigner, partly because people of small ability tend to hate someone of great ability. His envious peers "could find no corruption in him, because he was trustworthy and neither corrupt nor negligent." They were exasperated, but there was one possibility open: "We will never find any basis for charges against this man Daniel unless it has something to do with the law of his God" (Dan. 6:4–5).

Time to add a new word to your vocabulary: *satraps*. These were the provincial governors of the Persian empire. Chapter 6 tells us that the satraps and other officials went to King Darius with a flattering proposal: he should issue an edict stating that for the next thirty days, no one could pray to any god or man except Darius himself. True, this strikes us today as perfectly silly. Praying to a king? But remember that in ancient times, people considered their kings partly, or fully, divine. Powerful men often think they are gods, so Darius didn't put up much resistance to this request from his officials.

An interesting phrase occurs in this famous story: "the laws of the Medes and the Persians, which cannot be repealed" (Dan. 6:8). The plotters may have feared that the wise Daniel had so endeared himself to the king that Darius might give Daniel a loophole through this edict. But if his decree went out as one of the "laws of the Medes and the Persians," the king himself would never dare to revoke it.

Daniel was, of course, not happy to learn about the decree. But he had no intention of dishonoring his God. In his home, at the window that faced toward his homeland of Judea, he prayed to God three times a day, just as he had done before the decree took effect. His enemies saw him praying and went running gleefully to tattle to Darius. They reminded him of his new law, and he replied, "The decree still stands—in accordance with the laws of the Medes and Persians, which cannot be repealed" (Dan. 6:12).

Then they dropped the bomb: someone has dared to defy that decree, none other than Daniel himself. The envious plotters were elated, but the king was not. "He was greatly distressed; he was determined to rescue Daniel and made every effort until sundown to save him" (Dan. 6:14). But the officials would not let up: the decree had to be enforced, did it not?

So, very grudgingly, Darius gave the order: throw Daniel into a den of lions. The king wasn't exactly malicious about it; he said to Daniel, "May your God, whom you serve continually, rescue you!" (Dan. 6:16).

About those lions: they aren't found in the region today, but in ancient times kings kept them. They served not as zoo specimens, but to hunt in the royal parklands, and also as symbols of the king's own royal power. The "den" was probably a sort of cavern or cellar, with a small opening in its roof for lowering food to the lions, plus a small door at the bottom so the lions could be released at certain times. Lions are not normally man-eaters, but this story makes us assume the obvious: Daniel was sent into the den when the lions were hungry.

Things did not look good. A stone was shoved over the opening to the den, "and the king sealed it with his own signet ring." The king himself was quite disturbed, not able to eat or sleep that night. The next morning he rushed to the den and called to Daniel "in an anguished voice." To his great relief and surprise, Daniel answered him: "O king, live forever! My God sent his angel, and he shut the mouths of the lions. They have not hurt me, because I was found innocent in his sight" (Dan. 6:17, 20–22).

Whew. All was well. The punishment had been administered as the "laws of the Medes and the Persians" required. Since the law had been followed, and Daniel had not be mauled and eaten, Darius had him taken from the den.

Darius was clearly impressed with the power of Daniel's God. He didn't exactly convert, but it was obvious to him that this Jewish God could not be trifled with. The envious court officials had opposed Daniel and his God, so Darius turned his wrath loose on them. They received the punishment they sought for Daniel: they were thrown into the lions' den—not only them, but their wives and children as well. "And before they reached the floor of the den, the lions overpowered them and crushed all their bones" (Dan. 6:25).

Darius issued another royal decree, praising the God of Daniel. And naturally, "Daniel prospered during the reign of Darius" (Dan. 6:28).

A nice story, yes? God saved a good man from disaster. He then thwarted his enemies in their plot and saw that they got the very punishment they intended for the good man. A godly received honor, and so did his God.

Any explanation for why the lions did not eat Daniel, but turned on his enemies and devoured them? Daniel attributed it to God's angel. If you believe miracles are possible, ask yourself the obvious question: why not?

Death by Eunuch

The painted Jezebel, and her theatrical ending

According to Webster's, a "jezebel" is "an impudent, shameless, or abandoned woman." The original Jezebel was the wife of wicked King Ahab of Israel. Her father was Ethbaal, the priest-king of Tyre and Sidon, and you might guess from his name that he was devoted to the god Baal. His daughter followed suit, and she was an enthusiastic supporter of the Baal cult in Israel. Her husband (who, we gather, was seriously henpecked) did not try to hold her back.

During Ahab's reign, there was a serious danger that the Baal religion might triumph completely over the worship of the true God of Israel. But Jezebel and the other Baal followers had a mighty opponent, the faithful prophet Elijah. We cover the confrontation between Elijah and the Baal cultists in another chapter.

Aside from her false religion, Jezebel was also responsible for Ahab's plot to confiscate the property of a man named Naboth, a plot that resulted in Naboth's death. The Naboth story, told in 1 Kings 21, reminded readers that people who followed after false gods always had low morals.

God was appalled at the wickedness of Ahab's family, and the instrument of divine punishment was one of Ahab's military men, a man named Jehu. God ordered the prophet Elisha to anoint Jehu king of Israel. At this time Ahab himself was already dead, but his equally wicked son Joram was on the throne. Elisha spoke on behalf of the Lord: "The whole house of Ahab will perish. I will cut off from Ahab every last male in Israel—slave or free . . . As for Jezebel, dogs will devour her on the plot of ground at Jezreel, and no one will bury her'" (2 Kings 9:8, 10).

Joram the king knew something was afoot. He rode out to meet Jehu

172

and asked him, "Have you come in peace?" Jehu gave a classic reply: "How can there be peace as long as all the idolatry and witchcraft of your mother Jezebel abound?" (2 Kings 9:22) Joram quickly concluded that Jehu had definitely *not* come in peace. He turned to flee but did not get far: Jehu shot an arrow that pierced his heart.

Jehu was in luck that day: Joram happened to be meeting with the king of Judah, Ahaziah—who was also his nephew, the son of Ahab's daughter Athaliah. In other words, the king of Judah was part of Ahab's wicked dynasty also. Jehu wasn't about to let him get away, and Jehu's men fatally wounded him in his chariot.

A busy day's work: death to Ahab's son, the king of Israel, and to Ahab's nephew, the king of Judah. Inevitably Jehu turned his attention to Ahab's widow, the Baal lady herself, Jezebel. She was in the city of Jezreel, and she had already heard of the murders of her son and nephew. Things seemed to be favoring Jehu, and she knew she was next on his hit list.

But the wicked lady was going to go out with a flourish. We read that "she painted her eyes, arranged her hair and looked out of a window" (2 Kings 9:30). If she was going to be assassinated, she was going to be beautiful when it happened.

"As Jehu entered the gate, she asked, 'Have you come in peace, Zimri, you murderer of your master?'" (2 Kings 9:31) Her last words on earth were a slap at Jehu's conspiracy. Zimri was the royal official who had assassinated an earlier king of Israel—then lived to reign only seven days himself. Jezebel was taunting Jehu, letting him know that conspirators must live in fear of another conspiracy.

Jezebel's son and nephew had died by arrow. Jezebel's fate would be different. Jehu called up to the palace window and asked who was on his side. Some of the palace eunuchs looked down at him. Jehu ordered them to throw her down. We gather they merely shoved her out the palace window. "And some of her blood spattered the wall and the horses as they trampled her underfoot" (2 Kings 9:33).

Jehu despised the wretched Jezebel, but knowing she was of royal blood, he did order his men to bury her properly. "But when they went out to bury her, they found nothing except her skull, her feet, and her hands" (2 Kings 9:35). Dogs—not cuddly household pets, but wild mongrels of the streets—had devoured her body. So much for royal Jezebel.

Elijah and Elisha had both prophesied a horrible end for her, and the prophecies came true.

Jehu was not finished with killing, for there were still plenty of Ahab's clan left.

As for Jezebel, she is not an easy person for us to sympathize with. Reared in the coastal cities of Tyre and Sidon, she thought of her homeland as a civilized place, while Israel was a backwards country in the interior—"the sticks," you might say. Married to Ahab, she thought it her duty to get rid of the worship of Israel's tribal god and replace it with her native religion of Baal worship. She was, so she thought, doing Ahab and his nation a favor. If she had to hunt down prophets like Elijah and eliminate them, so be it.

She had to remind her husband that as king he ought to have supreme power—so if he wanted the property belonging to Naboth, well then, seize it, and forget all about property rights, individual rights, whatever. She had a high opinion of herself, her religion, and the rights of rulers.

And she ended up being shoved out a window by two eunuchs, with her body gobbled by the dogs that roamed the streets. So much for worldly power and false religion.

Not Exactly Cupid's Arrow

A swift (and brutal) punishment for mixed marriage

You used to hear the phrase *mixed marriage* fairly often, and it referred to a marriage in which the two people were of different religions. You don't hear it much any more because we are taught to be "tolerant" and "nonjudgmental." Perhaps more importantly, we are taught that religion isn't really all that important—just a sort of personal preference, like choosing one brand of coffee over another.

You certainly won't find that attitude in the Bible. Mixed marriages were frowned on, and in the later part of the Old Testament, in the book of Ezra, we see that it became a standard practice in Israel to avoid mixed marriages altogether (see Ezra 10). There was a fear that a spouse who served a different god (or gods) would lead the worshiper of the true God astray. It was a reasonable fear, for it happened continuously throughout Israel's history.

Solomon, the wise and wealthy king of Israel, the man who built the glorious temple for God in Jerusalem, started out his reign as God's man. But his many wives and concubines, who came from different nations and cultures, wanted to worship their own gods, so Solomon built temples to please them. Solomon watered down his own faith (1 Kings 11:4), and so did every other person who married a worshiper of false gods.

Keep something in mind: religion involves more than prayer to a certain god. It involves morality, too, and the various religions of the ancient world were not known for their high moral standards. Most of the false religions were some form of fertility cult, meaning the people worshiped gods and goddesses of fertility—and "worship service" was often just another term for "orgy."

You see this neatly summed up in Numbers 25:

> While Israel was staying in Shittim, the men began to indulge in
> sexual immorality with Moabite women, who invited them to the sac-
> rifices to their gods. The people ate and bowed down before these
> gods. So Israel joined in worshiping the Baal of Peor. And the LORD's
> anger burned against them. (Num. 25:1–3)

Sex and religion—a bad (but very enticing) combination. The loose
women of Moab enticed the Israelite men, who were supposed to worship only God, into Baal worship. And why not? Instead of serving a holy
God who demanded high moral standards, they could worship Baal,
whose cult was blatantly sexual. Give men the choice of church or
brothel, and many men will happily choose the brothel.

Seeing that many of Israel's men were making this choice, God gave
Moses an order: execute them. While this order was being carried out,
the more moral and sensitive among the Israelites were literally weeping
for shame.

But one lecherous man had no shame at all. In full view of everyone,
he headed for his tent, with one of the foreign women in tow. This was
too much for Phinehas, the grandson of the high priest, Aaron. Phinehas
grabbed a spear and headed for the man's tent. Punishment was swift
and brutal: "He drove the spear through both of them—through the Israelite and into the woman's body" (Num. 25:8). Two adulterers, one
spear.

Gory, yes, but the Lord recognized that Phinehas was a man of
honor. He approved of Phinehas's act and told Moses that Phinehas
would be rewarded: "He and his descendants will have a covenant of a
lasting priesthood, because he was zealous for the honor of his God"
(Num. 25:13).

God was true to his promise, for Phinehas's descendants held the
priesthood for centuries, until the days of King Herod. Later generations
remembered Phinehas as a man of faith, as we see from his favorable
mention in Psalm 106:30.

The Bible names the man and the woman that Phinehas killed, and
for a reason: both were high on the social scale. The man, Zimri, was the
son of one of the chiefs of the tribe of Simeon. The woman, Cozbi, was
daughter of one of the chiefs of Midian. By naming them the Bible drives
home a point: it wasn't just the riffraff engaging in Baal worship (and

blatant sexual immorality), but the upper crust, too. If Zimri had gotten away with his sin, it would have sent the message that Baal worship and adultery were fine, since a son of one of the "best families" was a flagrant adulterer.

As in other Old Testament stories, all this impresses our modern minds as rather barbaric. We tend to make light of sexual sins, just as we take choices of religion pretty lightly. No one today would advocate murdering adulterers with spears (especially while they are in the act). But the story is a reminder that morality matters, that Israel's God wanted his people to live a higher life than the people around them.

Tamar and the World's First ID Bracelet

Giving a new meaning to "family relations"

Ever heard the term *bowdlerized?* Back in the 1800s, a man named Thomas Bowdler went through the works of William Shakespeare and removed all the parts he thought might cause people to blush. The result was his *Family Shakespeare.* He did the same thing to the Old Testament, and one of the sections he cut was Genesis 38. This is, to put it mildly, a pretty bizarre story, and it definitely could cause a blush. It is also oddly placed, for it falls smack in the middle of the account of Joseph (the "coat of many colors" guy).

We won't quote the whole chapter here, but here is a nutshell summary: Judah, one of the twelve sons of Jacob, fathered two out-of-wedlock sons. Both sons, Er and Onan, were so wicked the Lord killed them both. Er's widow, Tamar, went to live in Judah's house. Later she disguised herself, and Judah, thinking she was a prostitute, hired her. (He offered as a fee a young goat.)

Naturally she became pregnant by her father-in-law. Her ruse was revealed, and Judah felt ashamed about having had relations with his own daughter-in-law.

Sounds like a segment from the worst type of daytime TV talk shows, yes? The sordid tale has a curious twist at its end:

> When the time came for her to give birth, there were twin boys in her womb. As she was giving birth, one of them put out his hand; so the midwife took a scarlet thread and tied it on his wrist and said, "This one came out first." But when he drew back his hand, his brother came out, and she said, "So this is how you have broken out!" And he was

named Perez. Then his brother, who had the scarlet thread on his wrist, came out and he was given the name Zerah. (Gen. 38:27–30)

That name *Perez* explains why Genesis included this odd story: Perez became the ancestor of the leading clan in the tribe of Judah—the ancestor of David and all the later kings of Israel. The part about the "ID bracelet" (the scarlet thread) strikes us as silly—until you remember how much value these people placed on the firstborn son. We know that twins are conceived at the same time, but for the ancient Israelites, the first twin to come from the womb was still officially the firstborn son, with all the rights and privileges.

The story actually has a bit of humor: the twin Zerah put his hand out of the womb, the thread was tied on—but it was the other twin, Perez, who made the full exit first.

Perez, child of Judah and his daughter-in-law, was the ancestor of Israel's kings—and also of Jesus. Perez was not exactly conceived under the most respectable circumstances, which is a reminder that good people don't necessarily have perfect people as their ancestors.

The Unheard-of
Sin of Gibeah

When sleeping in the park might have been better

Humankind has committed its share of sexual sins, as well as crimes of violence. The Bible never tries to whitewash these sins, and for that reason the whole Bible, or at least the Old Testament, ought to have a "Parental Advisory" warning label attached. Nowhere is that more true than Judges 19, which is a story worth reading, though not something one would want to read aloud to the kids at bedtime.

The chapter opens with the words "In those days Israel had no king." Those words occur more than once in the book. In fact, the book ends in this way: "In those days Israel had no king; everyone did as he saw fit" (Judg. 21:25). Put another way, there was no king, no centralized authority to keep order, so crime ran rampant. Judges 19 depicts one of the most abhorrent of those crimes.

The story starts out almost like a pleasant fairy tale: "Now a Levite who lived in a remote area in the hill country of Ephraim . . ." (Judg. 19:1). The Levite (a man from the tribe of Levi, that is) took a concubine from Bethlehem—the town that was the birthplace of both David and Jesus, but this was centuries earlier. The concubine went back to live with her family, the man followed to fetch her to his home, and eventually he, she, and the man's servant began the journey toward the Ephraim. Around sunset they decided to stop for the night in Gibeah.

Hospitality was highly valued in the ancient world. Though there were a few inns, most travelers chose to stay with people they knew, either family members or old friends. If you visited a strange town, you could usually count on some kind stranger taking you into his home.

But not in Gibeah. The Levite, his concubine, and his servant sat in the town square, hoping some hospitable soul would offer them shelter

180

for the night, but no one did. Finally, along came an old man—who happened to be from the same region as the traveling Levite. He invited the three into his home. (Nothing like folks from one's home territory!) The old man and his guests were eating and drinking and enjoying themselves, when suddenly the local thugs brought everything to a halt.

"Some of the wicked men of the city surrounded the house. Pounding on the door, they shouted to the old man who owned the house, 'Bring out the man who came to your house so we can have sex with him'" (Judg. 19:22).

Well, the three travelers had already learned that the people of Gibeah (the old man excepted) were not hospitable. Now they learned the locals were perverts as well.

The old man went outside and tried to reason with the locals. He asked them not to commit vile acts with the guest under his roof. Instead, would they settle for his own daughter, and for the Levite's concubine instead? The Levite sent the concubine outside. "And they raped her and abused her throughout the night, and at dawn they let her go. At daybreak the woman went back to the house where her master was staying, fell down at the door and lay there until daylight" (Judg. 19:25–26).

That morning the Levite found her lying at the door, with her hands on the threshold. When he spoke to her, she did not answer. She was dead.

If the story ended there, it would be sordid enough. But here is the finish: The Levite strapped her to his donkey and continued on home. Arriving there, he cut the dead body into twelve pieces and sent the pieces off to the various parts of Israel. "Everyone who saw it said, 'Such a thing has never been seen or done, not since the day the Israelites came up out of Egypt. Think about it! Consider it! Tell us what to do!'" (Judg. 19:30).

What, indeed? And you may be asking yourself another question: why was this disgusting, disturbing story even included in the Bible? It certainly wouldn't qualify as uplifting or inspiring.

In fact, it is in the Bible for a good reason: we need to know how low human beings can sink. We need to know what happens to people's morals and consciences when they forget God. The whole book of Judges is one long lesson in how the Israelites, God's chosen people, forgot God, worshiped false gods, and lapsed into the worst forms of immorality. At the end of Judges 19, when the Levite cut up his dead concubine and sent a piece to each tribe of Israel, the message was that the whole nation was implicated in the crime.

The Levite himself was not exactly a hero. He and the old man of Gibeah were both, by our standards, sexist, since they shoved the poor concubine out the door for the Gibeah thugs to use sexually. But neither the Levite nor the old man expected her to be mistreated to the point of death. The men of Gibeah, very inhospitable and very perverted, too, are the real villains of the story.

Centuries later, the prophet Hosea could mention the Judges 19 incident and expect his hearers to remember it: "Since the days of Gibeah, you have sinned, O Israel, / and there you have remained" (Hos. 10:9).

People of faith are right in trying to "accentuate the positive" in the Bible. But we need, on occasion, to force ourselves to read the darker passages, such as Judges 19. They are necessary reminders that the world can be a pretty grim place, that human beings can behave abominably toward each other. And if you think such deeds no longer occur, you don't know much about the modern world . . . or about human nature.

Rocking Out the Water

—

Talk to it, or hit it—the difference was huge

The Bible presents human beings warts and all, and with the single exception of Jesus, it presents no one as being flawless. That is to be expected, for the Bible is the book of God, not the book of Saintly Human Heroes. True, there are some admirable characters in it, real heroes of the faith, good role models. But all of them appear three-dimensionally, with all their faults and errors.

There are two reasons for this: those faults and errors were real, and the Bible authors wanted to make sure that God's people did not fall into worshiping mere humans. It is fine for us to read our children Bible stories and tell them to "Be like Daniel" or "Be like Moses." But we are probably missing the main point of the Bible, which is this: depend on God, and worship no one but him.

Now, to one of the best-known heroes of the faith, and one of the great men of history: Moses, the most important human figure in the Old Testament. His story is timeless, and in this book we look at several amazing events in his life, such as meeting God at the burning bush, the plagues on Egypt, the parting of the sea, the miraculous food known as manna, and so on. But one of the bizarre events in Moses' life had a tragic payoff afterward, something that made Moses' end almost a tragedy.

The Israelites were still in the wilderness, having left slavery in Egypt, and on their way (over a period of forty years!) to the promised land of Canaan. They griped constantly and seemed chronically ungrateful for the wonders God had performed on their behalf.

But to be fair, their life in the wilderness was no picnic. True, God was kind enough to provide them with food, but water (even more important to human life than food is) was not always easy to get. In chapter 20 of Numbers, the people were at a place called Kadesh and on the verge of rebelling against Moses and his brother Aaron, for there was no water. They resorted to their usual lament: "Why didn't you leave us in Egypt? Why did you have to bring us to this desert to die?"

Moses went to meet with the Lord at the Tent of Meeting, and the Lord told him how he would provide: "Speak to the rock before their eyes and it will pour out its water" (Num. 20:8).

Moses had learned that God always made good on his promises. If God said he would bring water from the rock when Moses spoke to it, it would happen just that way. So he and Aaron gathered in front of the rock. (Which rock? We aren't told, but we have to assume it must have been some noticeable rock formation.) Moses raised his arm and struck the rock twice with his staff. Water gushed out, and the people shut up (temporarily, anyway).

But alas and alack! Moses, the devoted servant of the Lord, had made a serious error. God's instructions had been simple enough: speak to the rock. Moses had struck it instead. The water came out, but God was displeased with Moses: "Because you did not trust in me enough to honor me as holy in the sight of the Israelites, you will not bring the community into the land I give them" (Num. 20:12).

The Bible does not tell us how Moses reacted to this. We can imagine it was like being hit with a sledgehammer. After all this time, after all these miracles, after enduring all this people's griping—Moses, their leader, would not enter the promised land, Canaan.

If you are like most readers, you are tempted to yell out, "That ain't fair!" To our way of thinking, no, it ain't. Moses had served God with all his heart. He had remained humble, even though he was the only human being who ever met God "face to face." And after all his loyalty and devotion to God and to the people of Israel, he would not enter Canaan—all because of the tiny detail of striking the rock instead of speaking to it. It makes God seem petty and nitpicky, doesn't it? You might be thinking that the really bizarre incident was not the water from the rock but the punishment God imposed on Moses.

If you are a really alert Bible reader, you might be thinking there was another incident where Moses brought water from a rock. That was much earlier, in Exodus 17, not long after the famous parting of the sea.

On that occasion, God did instruct Moses to strike the rock with his staff. Years and miles later, God changed his directions slightly: just speak to the rock. Moses disobeyed, and he paid a high price for it.

Let's replay the scene, and look at another detail in it: after God gave Moses the instructions to speak to the rock, Moses and Aaron went to the rock, and Moses addressed the people: "Listen, you rebels, must we bring you water out of this rock?" (Num. 20:10). Then he struck the rock, and the water flowed. Moses had spoken harshly to the people. We can sense sarcasm and bitterness in his words, and perhaps he even struck the rock angrily. In other words, he had changed the nature of the miracle: God had intended it to be a demonstration of his power and his care for the people. Moses' harsh words and striking the rock with his staff shifted the emphasis from God to the rebellious people.

This is one interpretation of what happened that day, and it has the benefit of making God look less unkind and Moses a little more at fault.

But though Moses did not enter Canaan, his ending was not really tragic. The last chapter of Deuteronomy tells us that Moses climbed Mount Nebo, on the border of Canaan, and at least got to see from afar the land his people would occupy. Moses died and was buried—not by human hands, but by God himself. And Deuteronomy ends with an affirmation that "no prophet has risen in Israel like Moses, whom the LORD knew face to face" (Deut. 34:10).

Jesus Cursing?

The Master, and that (literally) blasted fig tree

Sometimes we see what we wish to see. There was only one Jesus Christ, but there are many Jesuses in people's minds, because people tend to remember the details they like and forget those they don't like. Here in the twenty-first century, when we like the "sensitive man," we tend to think of Jesus as a "nice guy," the sweet fellow who stopped a crowd from stoning the adulterous woman. (People forget that important detail that afterward he told her, "Go and sin no more" [John 8:11 KJV].) In some people's minds, Jesus was like the "nice guy" of today—meaning he was "tolerant" and "nonjudgmental." An interesting Jesus, and not much like the real one.

Jesus did talk a lot about love—God's love for us, our need to love God, our need to love our neighbors. But this same Jesus also told parables about people being cast forever into "outer darkness" (Matt. 22:13 KJV) if they did not repent, and about an "everlasting fire" (Matt. 18:8 KJV) in which the wicked would be punished. For the Jesus of the Bible, God is love—and God is the great Judge also. Love—and judgment, too. Not either/or but both/and. Maybe we don't believe a "sensitive man" would want it both ways. But according to the Bible, Jesus did.

Jesus was, you recall, a miracle worker. He healed people, he cast out demons, he turned water into wine, he multiplied a few fish and loaves of bread to feed a huge crowd. Note that all these miracles were *compassionate*. They witnessed to Jesus' amazing power, but also to his love for people. Jesus did not go around doing miracles just to amuse or amaze people. His miracles always had a loving purpose.

Or *almost* always. Consider Matthew 21:19–21:

Seeing a fig tree by the road, he went up to it but found nothing on it except leaves. Then he said to it, "May you never bear fruit again!" Immediately the tree withered.

When the disciples saw this, they were amazed. "How did the fig tree wither so quickly?" they asked.

Jesus replied, "I tell you the truth, if you have faith and do not doubt, not only can you do what was done to the fig tree, but also you can say to this mountain, 'Go, throw yourself into the sea,' and it will be done."

We are tempted to say, "Poor tree!" Then we realize something else: Jesus, the loving Son of God, put a curse on an inanimate object. What happened to the "sensitive" Jesus we like so much? Nothing had happened. Jesus, who was fully human, had gone to the tree hoping to find figs, for the obvious reason he was hungry. He found no figs on it, and he took it as an opportunity to show his disciples his divine power.

And he told them that they could exercise such power—if they had enough faith, that is. They could even move mountains. ("Faith that can move mountains" is a phrase that has been in the Christian vocabulary a long time.)

But don't misunderstand what happened. We already said that Jesus didn't ordinarily use his power to amuse and amaze an audience. And when he told them they could move mountains, he didn't intend that they should go around rearranging the landscape—or putting curses on trees, either. By his own life he showed what the power of God was for— to heal and to help people. So the incident with the fig tree was just a demonstration to the disciples of the power that was at their disposal.

What he said proved to be true: his disciples, and later generations of believers, did do some truly amazing things. If they did not literally move mountains, they did things that were equally miraculous.

A Relative Matter

What happened after Lot's wife became a pillar of the community

Elsewhere in this book we look at the cities of Sodom and Gomorrah, the vice-saturated towns that God destroyed. One who fled the destruction was Lot, along with his wife and daughters. The family was told to flee and not look back. Lot's wife disobeyed and turned into a pillar of salt. A sad ending for her, and one that produced some unhappy results for the surviving members of the family, too.

For some reason Lot and the daughters did not settle in any nearby town. They went off to the mountains and lived in a cave. Apparently the time the family had spent in Sodom was proving to be an evil influence, for the older of his two daughters proposed a plan to her sister: since there were no men around there except Dad, she suggested getting him drunk and conceiving children by him. She didn't hatch the plan for purely sexual reasons; she and her sister both wanted children, as all women in the ancient world did.

"That night they got their father to drink wine, and the older daughter went in and lay with him. He was not aware of it when she lay down or when she got up" (Gen. 19:33). The following night, the younger daughter did the same thing. Both got what they wished, for both became pregnant by their father. Each had a son by him, and the two sons became the ancestors of the Moabites and the Ammonites.

Those tribal names may not mean much to you, but they meant a lot to the Israelites, for the Moabites and Ammonites were neighbor nations, both notorious for their idol worship, immorality, and frequent wars with Israel. Genesis 19 is telling us that those two immoral nations sprang from incest.

Not a very pretty story. It is also puzzling, because Genesis tells us

188

that God sent two angels to deliver the "righteous" (Lot and his family) from the destruction of Sodom. In this story of incest, neither Lot nor his daughters appear very righteous.

You might be skeptical about the story and wonder if the Israelites told it as a way of putting down their enemies, the Moabites and Ammonites. That is possible. But many scholars think those people themselves may have circulated the story—that is, they were actually proud of being descended from these take-charge women who were willing to do the unthinkable in order to produce children. From what we know of the Moabites and Ammonites, this might have been true.

Not much take-home value in this bizarre incident, except to remind ourselves that if we live among immoral people (such as the folk of Sodom), we and our children may absorb more from them than we realize.

Gabriel the Tongue-Stopper

Cat got your tongue—or an angel, maybe?

Angels suddenly became trendy in the 1990s, and still are. People were buying books about angels, plus angel figurines, and some malls even had entire stores devoted to angels. These were usually of the cute and cuddly variety—sort of "spiritual pets." They didn't usually bear much resemblance to the angels of the Bible, the divine messengers that are anything but cute and cuddly. Most often the Bible's angels either appear to be like regular humans, or their form is extremely intimidating. You would not make "spiritual pets" of the angels in the Bible.

The Bible mentions only two by name. One is Michael, the other is Gabriel. While Gabriel made an appearance in the book of Daniel, we remember him chiefly because of the major role he played in the events surrounding the birth of Jesus (see Luke 1). You may remember that he was the angel who visited the virgin Mary and told her she would bear the child Jesus—and with no human father involved in the process. Catholic and Orthodox Christians celebrate this visit every year on the holy day known as the Annunciation—on March 25, exactly nine months before Christmas, if you get the connection.

Before that famous visit to Mary, Gabriel had paid another visit to earth, to a priest named Zechariah. He and his wife, Elizabeth, were "upright in the sight of God, observing all the Lord's commandments and regulations blamelessly. But they had no children, because Elizabeth was barren; and they were both well along in years" (Luke 1:6–7).

In other words, they were lovely people but had no children, and they were too old to hope to have them. (Remember that childlessness was considered a terrible thing in those days.)

Zechariah was in the temple in Jerusalem, doing his official duties. "Then an angel of the Lord appeared to him, standing at the right side of the altar of incense." We aren't told what the angel looked like, nor how Zechariah knew it was an angel. But we know his reaction: "When Zechariah saw him, he was startled and was gripped with fear" (Luke 1:11–12).

The angel told him not to be afraid: in fact, he brought good news, for the aged Elizabeth would conceive and bear a son, whom they would name John.

> He will be great in the sight of the Lord. He is never to take wine or other fermented drink, and he will be filled with the Holy Spirit even from birth. Many of the people of Israel will he bring back to the Lord their God. And he will go on before the Lord, in the spirit and power of Elijah, to turn the hearts of the fathers to their children and the disobedient to the wisdom of the righteous—to make ready a people prepared for the Lord. (Luke 1:15–17)

Note the part about not drinking wine: the angel was saying that the child would be a Nazirite, totally dedicated to the Lord's service. If the words about Elijah puzzle you, recall that Elijah was the great prophet who never died but was taken into heaven in a chariot of fire. Jews in the New Testament period believed Elijah would return to earth someday to prepare people for the "day of the Lord."

All of this was great news, of course. But Zechariah seemed skeptical. "How can I be sure of this? I am an old man, and my wife is well along in years" (Luke 1:18). The angel announced that his name was Gabriel, and that he stood in the presence of God. Because Zechariah was doubtful about God's own messenger, he would not be able to speak until the child was born.

People in the outer part of the temple wondered why Zechariah was lingering inside. When he finally came out, he could not speak to them—which must have been frustrating, for a man who had just encountered an angel would surely wish to talk about it. The poor man was reduced to talking in sign language. But what the angel prophesied came true. Zechariah went home, and his wife conceived.

For nine months Zechariah remained mute. In fact, he remained so even after his son was born. Following Jewish tradition, the son was circumcised on the eighth day, also the day on which he would be named. The mute Zechariah remembered what the angel had said. So he wrote down the words "His name is John." From that moment he could speak again.

Friends and neighbors were awed by all these happenings, naturally. Men can remain fertile for decades, but most women do not, so Elizabeth's pregnancy and birthing were truly astonishing. So, for that matter, was Zechariah's muteness through all the months of his wife's pregnancy. And suddenly he could talk again, once he had named his son. People asked, "What then is this child going to be?" (Luke 1:66).

Zechariah knew already, for he remembered Gabriel's words about the child. Luke 1:67–79 contains the Song of Zechariah, in which the happy father praised God and predicted great things of this son of his old age.

You may already know that the child became the famous John the Baptist, the great wilderness prophet who preached repentance and baptized people in the Jordan River. Among those he baptized was a relative, the man called Jesus of Nazareth.

Why de Walls Come Tumblin' Down

Joshua's literally earth-shaking trumpet band

———

According to the old spiritual, "Joshua fit de battle of Jericho, and de walls come tumblin' down." Not quite true—actually, the walls came down first, then the fighting began. The story of the walls of Jericho is familiar, but it was a truly bizarre incident, and it deserves another look.

That old spiritual about Jericho is an "up" song, and Joshua is a very "up" book, full of optimism and faith in God. After forty long years of wandering through the wilderness after they left Egypt, the Israelites finally got to the promised land, Canaan. This was the turf God had promised them—all they had to do was move in and possess it.

The people already there, the various idol-worshiping and immoral tribes of Canaanites, weren't exactly pleased at this invasion. But the Israelites were tough—and more important, they had God on their side. So the book of Joshua is full of miracles, God using his power on behalf of his chosen people, Israel.

And one of the most memorable happened at the ancient, walled city of Jericho—a city that, so the archaeologists believe, might have been one of the oldest cities on earth.

The Jericho story began dramatically: Joshua saw a "man" (actually an angel) holding a drawn sword. The mysterious swordsman told Joshua he was commander of the Lord's army, and Joshua fell facedown on the ground. Like Moses at the burning bush, he was instructed to take off his shoes, for he was standing on holy ground. Joshua knew that heavenly aid was required to take Jericho, for the walled city was "tightly shut up because of the Israelites. No one went out and no one came in" (Josh. 6:1). The Israelites were expected—and not welcome.

But God told Joshua how to take the city, and it didn't involve an assault. The orders: have the Israelite soldiers march around the city once daily for six days. Have seven priests carry trumpets (made of rams' horns) in front of the ark of the covenant (the gold-covered chest that symbolized God's presence). On the seventh day, march around the city seven times while the priests blow the trumpets. Have all the people give a loud yell, and the city walls will fall. Attack it and occupy it.

You may have noticed a lot of sevens in all this. You may already know that seven is a significant number in the Bible. God created everything in six days, then ceased on the seventh, so seven symbolized completeness. Israel was required to rest on every seventh day. Mourning lasted seven days. Priests sprinkled the sacrificial blood seven times. Every seventh year was a "sabbatical" year. These are just a few examples. Seven in the Bible is almost a holy number, and it is the reason that even today people consider seven a lucky number.

Back to Jericho: when you read that the troops marched around the city, don't picture a large city like Chicago or Houston. Most of the "cities" in the Bible would be called "towns" (or "villages") today. Probably a complete circuit around Jericho was less than a mile (and remember, these Israelites were accustomed to a lot of walking).

The ark of the covenant played a role. Carried on poles by four men, the gilded box was a visible reminder that the invisible God was with them.

Put yourself in the place of the dwellers of Jericho, watching from the walls of the city. You had expected these Israelites, these people from the wilderness to besiege the city—or to give up and go away. Instead they were marching around the city in orderly fashion, carrying this weird gold chest. And they were completely silent. You might have found the whole sight comical—or unsettling.

On the seventh day, the Israelites were silent no more. Some of them were blowing trumpets. Joshua gave a command: "Shout! For the LORD has given you the city!" (Josh. 6:16). The people gave a loud holler—and the walls of Jericho collapsed. The Israelite men rushed in and captured the city.

They did more than capture it. They took all the valuables—silver and gold and such—and saved them for use in the Lord's worship. Then they burned the city, as God had commanded them. City walls were no match for the power of God.

You can choose to believe this story or not. Some skeptics have wondered if the walls might have fallen because of an earthquake at the moment the people shouted. Why not? God controls earthquakes. You can call the earthquake a natural phenomenon, but that would not explain why it just coincidentally happened when the Israelites were on hand.

If you think the whole story of the walls is pure fiction, the archaeologists believe otherwise. They have found that old Jericho had a double wall in those days, with the inner wall twelve feet thick, the outer one six feet thick. It appears that the walls had been violently toppled, and layers of charcoal and ash indicate the city had been burned at that time. Sounds remarkably like the Bible's account, doesn't it?

The fall of Jericho was the first really dramatic miracle after the Israelites entered Canaan. They had every reason to be optimistic, for it was clear to them that the God who had guided them through the wilderness and provided food for them there was still on their side. We, like they, can take heart from the knowledge that all the great miracles of God are not "ancient history." God is still our Protector, and there are more miracles ahead.

Smooth Man Versus Bear Man

You can always place your bets on the smoothie

In the ancient world, being the firstborn son carried a lot of privileges, something we talk about elsewhere in this book. Even in the case of twins, one twin had to come out of the womb before the other, so even though they had the same birthday (and same conception day as well), one was still considered the firstborn, the other ranking no higher on the family ladder than sons that were born years later.

Such was the situation with Isaac's twin sons, Esau and Jacob. Esau was first, and Jacob literally was holding on to Esau's heel when he came out of the womb. Oddly, the newborn Esau was covered with hair ("hairy" being the meaning of *Esau*). And "the boys grew up, and Esau became a skillful hunter, a man of the open country, while Jacob was a quiet man, staying among the tents. Isaac, who had a taste for wild game, loved Esau, but Rebekah loved Jacob" (Gen. 25:27–28). It was Daddy's boy versus Mama's boy, though since Esau was born first, there really was no contest.

But Jacob didn't see it that way. He wanted the birthright of the first-born son, and his mother, Rebekah, also wanted him to have those privileges. The opportunity came in an odd way: Esau came in from the hunt, ravenous with hunger, and Jacob happened to be cooking some stew. Esau asked for some, and Jacob, instead of replying, "Certainly, dear brother!" said, "First sell me your birthright."

Esau's stomach at that point was louder than his brain was. Rashly he agreed, lest he die of hunger. Just so he wouldn't renege later on, Jacob made him swear to give him the birthright. Genesis 25:34 says, "So Esau despised his birthright."

Interesting: Jacob had played a nasty trick, but the Bible faults Esau for being so foolish to sell his birthright for a quick helping of stew.

Curiously, Genesis never mentions this transaction again. In chapter 27 we learn that Isaac was blind and near to death, and was about to bestow his final blessing on his sons—the big blessing going to his beloved (and firstborn) Esau, naturally. The old man asked Esau to go and kill some game and fix him a fine meal before he died. Rebekah overheard this and contrived a plan: Jacob would disguise himself as Esau, bring his papa some food, then receive his blessing.

But what about Jacob's skin? Old blind Isaac would probably touch him, then he'd know it was Jacob, not the hirsute Esau.

Rebekah took goatskins and covered his hands and the back of his neck, and she dressed him in Esau's clothing. (Esau must have been one hairy dude.) Jacob took his father the food and claimed to be Esau. Isaac was a bit surprised that the hunter returned so quickly. He asked his son to come forward so he could touch him to determine that he was really Esau.

Isaac touched Jacob and said, "The voice is the voice of Jacob, but the hands are the hands of Esau" (Gen. 27:22). Isaac blessed him. They kissed, and Isaac, holding his son close, was pleased at the outdoorsy smell of Esau's clothes.

We don't take blessing too seriously now, but the Hebrews certainly did. Isaac's blessing had weight. He pronounced that his son's brothers would bow down to him, and that nations would serve him. Those who cursed him would be cursed, those who blessed him would be blessed. Serious stuff, and Jacob knew it.

After Jacob left, the real Esau returned. Poor Isaac trembled in agitation. Who was the guy who just left, the one calling himself Esau? Esau was furious. Jacob had already received the blessing, and people then believed you could not revoke such a thing. The deed was done.

Isaac could bestow another blessing on Esau, and he did. But he couldn't revoke his words to Jacob, so they stood: Esau would serve Jacob, and his descendants would be subject to Jacob's. Not surprisingly, Esau held a grudge against his crafty brother, and some of the later chapters of Genesis deal with Jacob's flight from Esau.

I've included the story of Jacob and the stew for two reasons: one, it actually happened; and two, it does excuse (sort of) the later behavior of

Jacob in tricking his father. That is, he was resorting to sneakery to get what Esau had already forfeited to him anyway.

Jacob was hardly an admirable character here, nor was his mother, Rebekah. Yet the author of Genesis was aware that Jacob became the father of the twelve sons that became the ancestors of the Israelites, so Jacob's story had to be told, even if Jacob was less than saintly. The real lesson of the Jacob-Esau stories has been preached on and commented on for centuries: don't be an Esau—that is, don't make rash mistakes as Esau did in selling his birthright.

Assyrian Death in Massive Doses

One angel, or a lot of rodents—and a lot of dead soldiers

The books known as 1 and 2 Kings could also be titled 1 and 2 Mostly Bad Kings. Israel and Judah both had their share of stinkers as rulers, but a few noble souls stand out. Among these was Hezekiah of Judah, whose story begins in 2 Kings 18.

It is a wonder he turned out well, for his father, Ahaz, was one of the nastier kings (see 2 Kings 16). Ahaz worshiped false gods and even sacrificed one of his own sons. Fearing attack from some neighboring nations, Ahaz had all the gold and silver stripped out of the Lord's temple and shipped off to the king of Assyria—in the hope that Assyria would help him fight off his enemies. In fact, he had the whole temple remodeled to please the king of Assyria.

By a funny coincidence, during Hezekiah's reign, the Assyrians completely conquered the northern kingdom of Israel, and then they resettled Israel with various foreigners. Assyria then turned its attention to the kingdom to the south, Judah. So poor Hezekiah had to face the might of King Sennacherib of Assyria.

Hezekiah was forced to do something he hated: buy off the Assyrians with money. (This was called "tribute." It meant that you paid the enemy to go away, and the price was always high.) Like his father, Hezekiah had to strip the Lord's temple of its valuables in order to pay the Assyrians.

But paying them off wasn't a permanent fix. Sennacherib still planned to conquer Judah. (Of course he did. He was no fool. He had a great scheme: threaten Judah, collect a lot of tribute, then conquer them anyway.) He sent some of his officials to Jerusalem to issue an ultimatum. They did so, not to Hezekiah personally, but to the whole city.

It was a kind of propaganda move, letting the citizens know that they were fools to resist mighty Assyria. The message: *Give up, you losers, and don't let King Hezekiah persuade you that you can win, or that God is on your side.*

Hezekiah was distressed at all this, but he had a good counselor at his side, the prophet Isaiah. The prophet had a message from the Lord: *Don't let these Assyrians rattle you, everything will be all right.* Reassuring, comforting words. But then Hezekiah got another message from the Assyrians: *Don't try to resist, for we Assyrians conquer everything in our way.* Hezekiah laid this message on the altar in the temple. Then he prayed for deliverance.

The king got another message from Isaiah, a long prophecy found in 2 Kings 19: Isaiah foretold that the Assyrians would never enter Jerusalem. Though they were a fierce and mighty empire, they would never even shoot an arrow into the city. Judah would prevail, for "the zeal of the LORD Almighty will accomplish this" (v. 31).

God's prophets can see further than most ordinary people can. At the time Isaiah uttered his words, some folks must have laughed, for the Assyrians seemed to be holding all the cards. They seemed invincible.

We get this short, strange, puzzling description of what followed Isaiah's prediction: "That night the angel of the LORD went out and put to death a hundred and eighty-five thousand men in the Assyrian camp. When the people got up the next morning—there were all the dead bodies! So Sennacherib king of Assyria broke camp and withdrew"(2 Kings 19:35–36).

As well he might. Hezekiah's God was more powerful than the Assyrians thought.

Pause a moment and consider this passage: 185,000 Assyrian soldiers slain by the "angel of the LORD." Really? What actually happened? Did some winged creature come down and strike them all with a sword? Not necessarily. God could well have sent some kind of plague on the army, causing sudden and massive death—and people at that time would attribute that to "the angel of the LORD"—which is another way of saying "the power of God."

Whatever caused the deaths, we do know for a historical fact that Sennacherib really did break camp and leave. The Greek historian Herodotus relates that mice overran the army at that time—and mice and other rodents were carriers of the notorious bubonic plague. Consider the irony: the fearsome Assyrian army, done in by an army of rodents.

What about Sennacherib himself? Thousands of his men died, but he escaped unharmed, right? Yes, but not for long. After he returned to the Assyrian capital, Nineveh, he had a fateful encounter: "One day, while he was worshiping in the temple of his god Nisroch, his sons Adrammelech and Sharezer cut him down with the sword, and they escaped to the land of Ararat. And Esarhaddon his son succeeded him as king" (2 Kings 19:37).

Again, the historical records support what the Bible says: his own sons murdered Sennacherib, then fled to the land of Ararat, and another son, Esarhaddon, was the new king.

One lesson is clear enough: there are no invincible nations or individuals in this world. Evil conquerors do not always get their just desserts in this world, but sometimes they do, as the Assyrians learned.

There is another lesson here too, a political one: don't try to appease a power bent on conquering. Hezekiah's foolish father Ahaz had kissed up to Assyria, hoping Assyria would never try to conquer Judah—and look what happened. The nations of Europe learned the same lesson in trying to appease Hitler in the 1930s: tyrants cannot be appeased, they can only be resisted. Happily for Judah in Hezekiah's reign, God proved to be the great Resister of evil empires.

A Truly Heavenly Spa

But no special concessions for the handicapped . . .

You may have heard of Bethesda, Maryland, a suburb of Washington. It was named for a site in Jerusalem with a very appropriate moniker, for *Bethesda* means "house of mercy." It happened to be the sight where one of Jesus' great miracles of healing occurred.

John 5 tells us that Jerusalem had a pool named Bethesda, surrounded by five covered colonnades. That detail is important, because for centuries people believed that John's Gospel was far more fiction than fact, with little basis in history or reality. But archaeologists have found the actual pool of Bethesda with its five covered colonnades, just as John described it.

John says that the blind, the lame, and paralyzed used to lie in these porches, waiting for the waters of the pool to move. From time to time an angel would come down and "trouble the waters," and the first person to enter the pool afterward would be healed of whatever his affliction was.

It happened that when Jesus came by, one poor man who had been an invalid for thirty-eight years was there, waiting for his chance to get into the waters. So far someone had always beat him to it. We don't know how long he had been waiting (not the whole thirty-eight years, probably). But his wait was over. Jesus told him to get up, pick up his mat, and walk.

It happened to be the Sabbath, and some of the Jewish authorities who witnessed what occurred were catty enough to tell the man that it was unlawful for him to carry his mat on the Sabbath. (The Jewish law prohibited them from carrying "burdens" on the Sabbath.) The man simply replied that the man who healed him had told him to carry his mat.

The Jews wanted to know who this fellow was, but by that time Jesus had slipped away into the crowd.

We include this story here not because of the healing but because of that mysterious pool. Was there really an angel that came down and disturbed its waters, or was that how the local people understood it? Most of the oldest copies of the Gospel of John don't include the verses that mention the angel, so there is some doubt about whether they were originally part of the Gospel.

We can't rule out the possibility of the power of suggestion—that is, some of the "ailing" people's sicknesses may have only been in their heads, and since they believed they would be cured if they entered the waters, they were. Another possibility: the pool was some kind of mineral spring that had genuine healing properties. What the people took to be an angel disturbing the waters might have been a sort of "belch" produced by the underground source of the waters. This "belch" might have temporarily introduced more of the healing minerals into the pool.

The story was not included in John's Gospel to satisfy our curiosity about the pool, of course. The point was that Jesus was the great Healer, the hope of all who had been untouched by the world's "natural" cures. And Jesus, quite unlike the pool, provided spiritual as well as physical healing. He still does.

Isaiah's Temple Trip

Six-winged, and possibly shaped like serpents

Do angels have wings? Based on the Bible, the answer is "Usually not." At times people in the Bible entertain "angels unawares" (Heb. 13:2 KJV), and we can assume people would definitely be aware of creatures with wings. In many angelic encounters, the angels appeared to be ordinary humans. In these cases, the person who met the angel somehow *knew* this was a messenger from the Lord, and not because it possessed wings.

But one particular type of angel did have wings. These were the *seraphs*, or *seraphim*. Their name means "burning ones," and the only time the Bible mentions them is in Isaiah 6, the famous chapter that describes the commissioning of the prophet. Isaiah was in the Jerusalem temple. He saw the Lord himself on a high throne, with a long robe that filled the temple.

> Above him were seraphs, each with six wings: With two wings they covered their faces, with two they covered their feet, and with two they were flying. And they were calling to one another:
> "Holy, holy, holy is the LORD Almighty;
> the whole earth is full of his glory." (Isa. 6:2–3)

(Obviously this passage is the source of that wonderful old hymn, "Holy, Holy, Holy.") The seraphs' voices must have been powerful—literally earthshaking, for the temple trembled, and the air was filled with smoke.

Poor Isaiah was overcome with awe. He cried out, "Woe to me! I am ruined! For I am a man of unclean lips, and I live among a people of un-clean lips, and my eyes have seen the King, the LORD Almighty" (Isa. 6:5).

Well, if your lips are unclean, they need purifying, and what better purifier than fire? So one of the seraphs used a pair of tongs and picked a live coal from the altar fire—and touched Isaiah's lips with it. This, the seraph said, purged his guilt and his sin away.

Then God himself called out, "Whom shall I send? And who will go for us?" And Isaiah uttered his famous reply: "Here am I. Send me!" (Isa. 6:8). Thus we learn how one of the best-loved, most-read prophets in the Bible got his start.

A nice story, isn't it—and rather bizarre, too. We can probably as-sume that what Isaiah saw was actually a vision, that a live coal didn't lit-erally touch his lips. Isaiah did not describe what the Lord himself actually looked like (pious Jews generally avoided making images of God, even in words). He did describe the seraphim, but all we know is that they had six wings—two for flying, two covering their faces, two covering their feet. Whether their bodies were basically human in shape is not revealed.

We noted earlier that the name *seraphs* does not appear elsewhere in the Bible, but that is not quite true: in Numbers 21 it occurs, but it refers to the "fiery serpents" that bit many of the Israelites in the wilder-ness. It is quite possible that the seraphs in Isaiah's vision were like six-winged serpents.

The seraphs are not the main point of the story: the holiness of God is. The young Isaiah had an experience in which it hit him full force that God was wonderful and holy, while people were evil. But instead of wal-lowing in despair and self-loathing, he went forth as a prophet of God.

Dropping Dead, After a Deadly Drop

That nameless (and lethal) woman with a millstone

In the book of Judges, Gideon is one of Israel's great heroes. Unfortunately, he had a rather nasty (and very ambitious) son named Abimelech, who came darn near to being Israel's first king. Only one person wanted him as king, and that was Abimelech himself. He was a legend in his own mind. But like many proud people in the Bible, he met an unpleasant end.

His career started on a bloody note: he murdered all seventy of his brothers, except one who managed to escape. (If you're skeptical about seventy brothers, yes, it was possible—not all by the same mother, of course.) Seeing that Abimelech was not a man to mess with, the people of Shechem made him king—and not out of any sense of affection.

Judges 9:22 says that "Abimelech had governed Israel three years"—which doesn't mean he was officially the king of the whole nation, but that he was probably top dog among many other dogs. And some of those dogs were jealous of his power, so revolts broke out. In the course of the fighting, Abimelech ended up torching his own city of Shechem. He and his men piled up tree branches outside the town's main battle tower and set them on fire.

He hoped to do the same thing in the town of Thebez, but something got in his way—a woman, to be specific. As he was approaching the town's tower to burn it, "a woman dropped an upper millstone on his head and cracked his skull" (Judg. 9:52).

He didn't die immediately. "Hurriedly he called to his armor-bearer, 'Draw your sword and kill me, so that they can't say, "A woman killed him."' So his servant ran him through, and he died" (Judg. 9:54). Oh, the things men do to save face—he knew he would have died from his head injury, but technically he died by the hand of a man, his own armor-bearer.

A millstone, by the way, was a large stone used for grinding grain into flour. There were two, an upper and a lower, big stone wheels that revolved on each other and ground up the grain. They were heavy and definitely could kill someone if dropped right on the head. The woman who dropped it was stout, to say the least (and gutsy to boot).

The Abimelech story illustrates a moral the Bible states many times: the violent often come to violent ends. Abimelech, unlike his father, Gideon, had no interest in saving Israel from foreign oppressors. He wanted only to rule, to fly the pennants of his pride, and such men are dangerous, as he proved by putting his own family members to death. His was a horrible death, but he is not a character who deserves our sympathy.

The Lord Giveth,
the Lord Taketh

The near-slaughter of Abraham's only boy

Abraham is one of the chief figures in the Old Testament, the "father of the faithful" (as he is often called) who was the physical and spiritual ancestor of the Israelites. Later, both Christians and Muslims looked to him as a spiritual role model. (He is *Ibrahim* to Muslims.)

Abraham's story appears in Genesis 12–25. It began when God called him from his pagan homeland of Ur to live in Canaan. God promised him that his many descendants would prosper if they served only the true God.

That prospect seemed unlikely, as Abraham's beautiful wife Sarah had never had children and was then too old to bear them. But this is one of many cases in the Bible where a woman who was past childbearing age was able to conceive—thanks to the power of God, of course. She bore the boy, Isaac (the name means "laughter," for everyone was pleased at this amazing birth).

So old Abraham finally had a son, and it seemed he might be able to live up to the meaning of his name ("father of a multitude"). But then, suddenly and with no explanation, God gave an order to the loyal Abraham: "Take your son, your only son, Isaac, whom you love, and go to the region of Moriah. Sacrifice him there as a burnt offering on one of the mountains I will tell you about" (Gen. 22:2). Abraham, the role model for those who trust in God no matter what, obeyed the order.

According to Genesis, the boy Isaac asked his father why there were wood and fire, but no lamb for a sacrifice. Abraham's answer was designed to bring a tear to the reader's eye: "God will provide." Abraham bound the boy to the altar and had raised up his knife to kill him—when the voice of an angel stopped him by saying, "Do not lay a hand on the boy. Do not do anything to him. Now I know that you fear God, because you have not withheld from me your son, your only son" (Gen. 22:12). Then the angel said that because of Abraham's faith, God would surely bless him. The sacrifice did take place—not with Isaac, but with a ram that was caught in a thicket nearby.

Quite a story, yes? And quite bizarre, too. Why would a loving, compassionate God test Abraham in this way? The answer ought to be obvious: to find out if he was as loyal as he seemed. He was, though we can only imagine what flashed through his mind as he raised the knife over his only child.

And what about Isaac's mind? He was probably terrified—but perhaps not, for perhaps he was aware that plenty of people in that part of the world did sacrifice their children, their firstborn in particular. The Israelites never did sacrifice children, finding the practice horrible. Some people believe that this story of the ram being substituted for Isaac was a signal from God that humans must never be sacrificed, only beasts.

A million sermons have been preached on this story, and rightly so. "If we all had as much faith as Abraham." Whatever we may think of God's test of Abraham, we have to admit that the man was definitely not lacking in trust.

Zeke and the
Extraterrestrials

———

The weirdest incident in the whole Bible, no contest

In the late 1960s and early 1970s, a new (and weird) publishing trend arose: books claiming the Bible was full of stories about encounters with aliens. Author Erich von Daniken had a runaway bestseller with his *Chariots of the Gods* (which is still in print), a book claiming that Israel's ark of the covenant was really a transmitter that received messages from extraterrestrial beings. But more famously, von Daniken claimed that the "living creatures" described in chapter 1 of the book of Ezekiel were actually alien spacecraft.

Josef Blumrich, a scientist, set out to debunk von Daniken—then changed his mind and wrote his own book, *The Spaceships of Ezekiel.* These two books were not the end of this disturbing new trend of attributing all the bizarre events in the Bible to aliens, not to God.

Your author doesn't happen to believe that Ezekiel ever saw alien spacecraft—but I will admit that Ezekiel 1 does describe something so otherworldly that it is no surprise that an unbeliever might take it for a "close encounter."

Let's let the prophet speak for himself:

> I looked, and I saw a windstorm coming out of the north—an immense cloud with flashing lightning and surrounded by brilliant light. The center of the fire looked like glowing metal, and in the fire was what looked like four living creatures. In appearance their form was that of a man, but each of them had four faces and four wings. Their legs were straight; their feet were like those of a calf and gleamed like burnished bronze. Under their wings on their four sides they had the hands of a man. All four of them had faces and wings, and their wings

touched one another. Each one went straight ahead; they did not turn as they moved. (Ezek. 1:4–9)

Note that the creatures had four faces each. Ezekiel went on to say that the faces were those of a human, a lion, an ox, and an eagle. Preachers and Bible scholars have had fun trying to interpret what those four faces meant—though they will never agree on it.

We won't quote the entire chapter here. It mentions that the "living creatures" moved around via something made like a wheel within a wheel. The chapter ends with Ezekiel believing he had seen the Lord himself seated on a sapphire throne. Ezekiel fell facedown in awe. From that point on, the book becomes more like the other prophets' books, with the Lord commissioning Ezekiel to speak on his behalf in order to set the people on the right path.

Ezekiel 1 is a long chapter, and full of detail. It is worth a read, but don't expect to understand it, and for that matter, don't expect to benefit from it spiritually. We really have no idea what the prophet saw, though we can agree with the UFO believers that Ezekiel really did see "extraterrestrials"—creatures not from earth, that is. Jews and Christians have usually believed that the prophet was seeing some of God's angels, not beings from another galaxy.

Ezekiel had this strange encounter in Babylon, where he and many other Jews had been deported after the Babylonians conquered Judah. The Babylonians, like most ancient countries, worshiped many gods, and they had many idols, often depicting the gods as a mixture of human and animal body parts. Some readers have suggested that Ezekiel had a vision of these idols coming to life—but at the end of the vision, he saw the true God on a throne above all the others.

Ezekiel and other devout Jews had always believed that God's "seat" was in the temple in Jerusalem. But the Babylonians had burned that temple and deported the Jews. In his vision he saw that God's throne was everywhere—even in pagan Babylon. The wheels in the vision seem to indicate mobility—God can get around, traveling like the wind. So you might say the wheels were a symbol of God's omnipresence: he can be everywhere because of this supernatural form of transport. The rims of the wheels were "full of eyes" (Ezek. 1:18), which is pretty easy to interpret: God is not only everywhere, but he saw everything.

Again, it is easy to get caught up in all these details, and many people have done so. That certainly was not Ezekiel's aim. Like the other prophets, he wrote only for the glory of God, and that seems to be the sole aim of chapter 1: impressing the reader with this basic fact, that God is truly awesome.

We don't know why God chose to reveal himself to Ezekiel in this bizarre fashion. In the commissioning of the prophet Isaiah, that prophet saw God on his throne in the temple of Jerusalem, where the seraphim (six-winged angels) were flying about and crying, "Holy, holy, holy." But Isaiah's vision was pretty tame stuff compared to what Ezekiel saw. Perhaps the prophet, stuck in this foreign land and probably feeling sorry for himself and his fellow Jews, needed this kind of bizarre jolt to get his career as a prophet going.

Perhaps we all need to reread Ezekiel 1 occasionally—not to wrack our brains wondering what all the details mean, but to get the overall impression of what Ezekiel saw, the glory and "otherness" of the Almighty.

Israel's King, Naked (But Not Really)

—

Saul in ecstasy, but not dressed for dinner

In English Bibles, you find the word *naked* many times, but it doesn't always mean *stark* naked. Genesis says Adam and Eve were naked and not ashamed, and we can definitely assume that they were absolutely bare. And Noah, caught naked and tipsy by his son, was most likely bare also.

But on occasion the Bible described a man as "naked" if he was, say, down to his loincloth (that is, the ancient equivalent of undershorts). The great prophet Isaiah walked around "naked" (but not totally) for three years (Isa. 2:3), and so did another prophet, Micah (Mic. 1:8), both of them underdressed as a way of lamenting their people's sins. The apostle Peter was caught "naked" while fishing (John 21:7)—not nude, but down to the minimal clothing.

And then there was Israel's first king, the tall and handsome Saul. On two occasions in Saul's career he fell into the company of a band of prophets, and he joined them in their prophesying. Let's explain: this wasn't a bunch of people getting together and predicting things. They were a group caught up in religious ecstasy, praising God, and probably shouting and dancing as well. (This has come back into style with the charismatic movement of recent years.)

Apparently such religious enthusiasm was not Saul's usual style, as 1 Samuel 10:11 reveals: "When all those who had formerly known him saw him prophesying with the prophets, they asked each other, 'What is this that has happened to the son of Kish? Is Saul also among the prophets?'" (Kish was Saul's father, of course.) This occurred soon after the prophet and judge Samuel anointed Saul and predicted that the Spirit would

213

come upon Saul and he would be "changed into a different person" (1 Sam. 10:7).

This happened a second time, and the timing was odd, to say the least: Saul was in pursuit of David, his rival, and hoping to kill him. Saul learned David was hiding out at a place called Naioth, and he sent his men there to capture David. But the Spirit moved Saul's men and they began prophesying. Saul sent another group, and the same thing happened.

Then a third group, and finally Saul himself went, "but the Spirit of God came even upon him, and he walked along prophesying until he came to Naioth. He stripped off his robes and also prophesied in Samuel's presence. He lay that way all that day and night" (1 Sam. 19:23–24).

But the well-beloved old King James Version reads differently, saying that Saul "lay down naked all that day and all that night." So many generations of Bible readers got this image of the king of Israel, ecstatic and naked, when really he was ecstatic and in his undies.

The story is important not because of Saul's clothing, of course, but because of the mysterious moving of God's Spirit. Saul was obviously not a man who let his better emotions run wild and free, but on at least two occasions he did, and 1 Samuel 19 shows that the Spirit changed him (temporarily, at least) from a man bent on murder to a man caught up in the Spirit.

Saul throwing off his robes and joining a band of religious celebrants is certainly more attractive than Saul the envious, angry, bitter man who hoped to kill his rival David. We should all pray for a world where people bent on doing evil could be so Spirit-possessed.

Outfoxing the Philistines

Samson and his infamous turn-tail trick

S amson is an unforgettable character, and a good example of God using a less-than-perfect human to do his will. God used Samson against those marauders known as the Philistines, and so perhaps it was no coincidence that Samson fell in love with a Philistine girl and married her, gaining him an entryway into the Philistines' territory.

In another chapter we look at Samson's wedding and the famous riddle he posed to the Philistines. After that incident, he decided to reclaim his Philistine wife, but his father-in-law would not admit him. In fact, the family thought Samson had cast the girl aside, so they had given her to another man.

The father-in-law offered Samson the girl's younger sister as a kind of consolation prize, but Samson did not accept. He was furious, and he saw this as a perfect excuse to do the Philistines some harm.

> So he went out and caught three hundred foxes and tied them tail to tail in pairs. He then fastened a torch to every pair of tails, lit the torches and let the foxes loose in the standing grain of the Philistines. He burned up the shocks and standing grain, together with the vineyards and olive groves. (Judg. 15:4–5)

Some Bible scholars think that the animals were actually jackals, not foxes. Whatever they were, they did tremendous harm.

And so did the Philistines. They laid the blame on Samson's wife and her father, so they punished them in the appropriate way: they burned them. This made Samson even madder, and he slaughtered some of them viciously. Tit for tat, and it didn't end there.

215

The Philistines camped among the Israelites and threatened revenge for what Samson had done. Fearing the worst, the Israelites went to Samson and asked would he please let them hand him over to the Philistines. He agreed, and they bound him with ropes.

But when he was about to be handed over, "the Spirit of the LORD came upon him in power. The ropes on his arms became like charred flax, and the bindings dropped from his hands. Finding a fresh jawbone of a donkey, he grabbed it and struck down a thousand men" (Judg. 15:14–15). (Oh, the uses that man could find for animals, even dead ones.)

All very bizarre, and yet a moral lesson is in there somewhere: God moves in mysterious ways. To deliver his people from the oppressive Philistines, God used the excitable, vengeful Samson. Samson does not appear as a "nice" person, nor even remotely spiritual. Yet God acted in him, using Samson's personal quarrels and grudges to get at the Philistines. When God wanted to punish a brutal, immoral people, he could do it himself (as at Sodom and Gomorrah, destroyed by fire from heaven), do it through the armies of Israel—or through unique individuals like Samson.

The Valley of Dem Bones,
Dem Bones, Dem Dry Bones

The prophet Ezekiel, stuck in the boneyard

T he knee bone's connected to the leg bone . . ." You've probably
heard the old spiritual about "dem dry bones" that "hear de word
of de Lord." Did you know it was based on the Bible? You'll find it
in chapter 37 of Ezekiel.

You might recall that the book of Ezekiel opens with one of the
weirdest visions a human being ever experienced. Ezekiel 37 is pretty
bizarre, too, but not quite so puzzling as chapter 1. And happily, chapter
37 is pretty clear about its meaning.

> The hand of the LORD was upon me, and he brought me out by the
> Spirit of the LORD and set me in the middle of a valley; it was full of
> bones. He led me back and forth among them, and I saw a great many
> bones on the floor of the valley, bones that were very dry. He asked me,
> "Son of man, can these bones live?"
>
> I said, "O Sovereign LORD, you alone know."
>
> Then he said to me, "Prophesy to these bones and say to them,
> 'Dry bones, hear the word of the LORD! This is what the Sovereign LORD
> says to these bones: I will make breath enter you, and you will come to
> life.'" (Ezek. 37:1–5)

Ezekiel did as he was told, and while he was still speaking, "there was
a noise, a rattling sound, and the bones came together, bone to bone."
Then the bones took on flesh, but the bodies didn't come to life until
God's breath entered them. They "stood up on their feet—a vast army"
(Ezek. 37:7, 10).

The reader doesn't have to puzzle long over the vision's meaning:

217

Then he said to me: "Son of man, these bones are the whole house of Israel. They say, 'Our bones are dried up and our hope is gone; we are cut off.'" Therefore prophesy and say to them: "This is what the Sovereign LORD says: O my people, I am going to open your graves and bring you up from them; I will bring you back to the land of Israel." (Ezek. 37:11–13)

In other words, God's people had had to endure the conquest of their nation, their temple ruined, their own deportation to far-off Babylon—but God had not forgotten them, and they would someday return home.

The vision is weird, indeed, but its message must have given hope to the Jewish exiles. For all they knew, they would never see their homeland again. But Ezekiel heard the word of the Lord: Israel's people would return home, the "dry bones" would come to life. This has happened again and again throughout history: In a season of "spiritual dryness," God breathes new life into his people. Revival comes, often when it is least expected.

The Leprosy Lady

How rebellion can affect the complexion

Y ou have probably heard of leprosy, also known as Hansen's disease. It is a disfiguring skin affliction that also affects the eyes and throat and can even cause nerve damage. Lepers (people with leprosy, that is) develop reddish brown spots on the skin, which become thickened nodules. The skin falls away, leaving open sores. In some cases deformity and wasting of muscle tissue occurs. It doesn't sound pretty, and it wasn't.

It has been known and described since ancient times—but not cured, for no one was really sure of the cause, much less the cure. Only in the past hundred years have doctors been able to effectively treat and cure the ancient disease. The usual treatment in days past was to segregate the affected persons from the larger community. In fact, in mankind's long history, there has probably been no disease whose victims have been treated with such malice and neglect.

Part of this was due to the fear that it was contagious (which is understandable), and part to the fact that lepers were often hideous to behold. In other words, people have been extremely unkind to those who are disfigured by a disease they had no control over.

You'll find a lot of references to "leprosy" in the Bible, particularly in Leviticus 13–14, which has detailed rules for dealing with lepers. One problem with interpreting the Bible is that we aren't sure if leprosy—the Hansen's disease I've just described—is what the writers were referring to, or if they meant some other skin diseases. This was a prescientific age, and the ancient Israelites weren't exactly experts in dermatology. So when you run across the word *leprosy* in the Bible, be aware that it may be referring to actual leprosy, or to any other diseases that affected the skin noticeably.

In Moses' famous first encounter with God at the burning bush, God gave Moses a miraculous sign of his power: he told Moses to place his hand inside his cloak, and when he withdrew it, "it was leprous, like snow" (Exod. 4:6). We can assume from this description that his skin was temporarily whitened—which is not usually a symptom of real leprosy. So you can see the terms *leprosy* and *leprous* got tossed about very loosely in those days. A "leper" could simply be someone with really creepy-looking skin.

We mentioned already that the usual treatment for such skin diseases was quarantining the person. Most skin diseases are not infectious but some are, so though the rules sound harsh to us, there was probably some merit in quarantine. "Command the Israelites to send away from the camp anyone who has an infectious skin disease or a discharge of any kind" (Num. 5:2). The person with the disease was "unclean," which explains this law from Leviticus 13:45–46:

> The person with such an infectious disease must wear torn clothes, let his hair be unkempt, cover the lower part of his face and cry out, "Unclean! Unclean!" As long as he has the infection he remains unclean. He must live alone; he must live outside the camp.

In other words, if you got leprosy, or some other noticeable skin ailment, and it didn't go away, you resigned yourself to a very unpleasant life. You can see why Jesus, the healer of lepers, made such an impression on these poor creatures.

The Bible mentions several important characters with leprosy, including one king of Judah (see 2 Chron. 26:19–21). There was also the foreigner Naaman, whom I discussed in an earlier chapter. But in the early pages of the Bible the most famous "leper" was Miriam, the sister of Moses and Aaron. You might recall that she played a role in hiding the infant Moses when the Egyptians were murdering the Hebrew children (Exod. 2), and she helped to procure Moses' own mother as a nurse for the baby when Pharaoh's daughter adopted him.

As an adult, Miriam was referred to as a "prophetess," and after the famous parting of the Red Sea, she led the women of Israel in a song of praise to God (Exod. 15:20–21). In other words, she was a very *good* character. But the Bible always looks at people warts and all, and even good characters can do bad things.

You see this in Numbers 12, where Miriam and Aaron were grumbling about the Cushite woman that Moses married. But we quickly learn that they were really grumbling out of jealousy: " 'Has the LORD spoken only through Moses?' they asked. 'Hasn't he also spoken through us?' " (v. 2).

God heard this envious murmuring and was not pleased. Speaking from "a pillar of cloud," he ordered all three of them to come out of the Tent of Meeting, and he ordered Miriam and Aaron to step forward. In no uncertain terms he reminded them that Moses was his own chosen prophet—a man faithful to him, and so close to him that the two "speak face to face" (Num. 12:5, 8). Since Moses was the Lord's chosen prophet, how dare they speak against him.

"When the cloud lifted from above the Tent, there stood Miriam— leprous, like snow. Aaron turned toward her and saw that she had leprosy" (Num. 12:10). Moses interceded for his rebellious sister, asking God to heal her. God said he would—but only after she was confined outside the Israelite camp for a full week. So the real punishment was not the leprosy—or whatever skin disease it was—but a week of being "grounded."

We have no idea what Miriam's skin affliction really was. Probably nothing that the medical books of today would recognize, for it was purely a temporary "pox" God had put on her for grousing about her brother. We learn later in the book of Numbers that Miriam died when the Israelites reached Kadesh, and she was buried there.

This bizarre incident of leprosy as punishment offends many readers. It shouldn't. Miriam and Aaron were grumbling against Moses, and there was a real threat to Moses' leadership if his own brother and sister were somehow against him. Rather than let their grumbling develop into a full-scale conspiracy, God chose to nip it in the bud with a dramatic demonstration of his power. Miriam got a sudden case of hideous skin, and for all she knew at the time, it might have been permanent. Aaron did not get the same punishment, but there is no doubt that what happened to his sister right before his eyes affected him.

Moses was not perfect, but Numbers 12 points out he was a very "humble" man (v. 3), which is quite remarkable for a man who had been closer to God than anyone who had ever lived. God could see that he had the right man for this awesome job of leading the quarrelsome, griping Israelite ex-slaves to their homeland in Canaan. He wasn't going to let Moses' own siblings start a rebellion against his chosen prophet.

Oh, by the way: the Hebrew name *Miriam* in time evolved into the name *Maryam*—the name of Jesus' mother and many other notable women in the New Testament. All those women would have been aware that they had been named for the famous sister of Moses—who had many virtues, despite her brief bout of griping and rebellion.

Peck Up Your Groceries

The Black Bird Catering Service (wide delivery zone)

Israel was God's chosen nation, but it had some really rotten kings. One of the worst, according to 1 Kings 16, was Ahab, who

did more evil in the eyes of the LORD than any of those before him . . . He also married Jezebel daughter of Ethbaal king of the Sidonians, and began to serve Baal and worship him. He set up an altar for Baal in the temple of Baal that he built in Samaria. Ahab also made an Asherah pole and did more to provoke the LORD, the God of Israel, to anger than did all the kings of Israel before him. (1 Kings 16:30–33)

But right after 1 Kings introduces these two nasties, Ahab and Jezebel, it introduces that remarkable man, Elijah the Tishbite, the great prophet of God. Elijah addressed wicked Ahab with a prediction: there will be a long drought, with no rain or even dew until Elijah says so. Then Elijah fled to the wilderness, lived by a brook, with food provided by . . . ravens.

Yes, ravens, those big black birds, relatives of crows, and looking like large versions of them. "The ravens brought him bread and meat in the morning and bread and meat in the evening, and he drank from the brook" (1 Kings 17:6).

Impossible? Not at all. Even if you don't believe in miracles, you might be aware that ravens, crows, jays, magpies, and all birds in that family are notorious thieves, snatching food from humans whenever they can. It is quite possible they could have snatched the food from people living not far from Elijah. But why would they have brought it to him? Well, there you do have to believe in miracles.

What prompted Elijah to leave this spot was the drought he had himself predicted. The brook had dried up, so he went to stay with a kindly widow, and he worked some miracles for her and her son. Wherever Elijah went, miracles followed.

The long drought did not end for years. It ended at an appropriate time, right after the famous contest between Elijah and the Baal prophets. And keep in mind how devastating this long drought was. The land was reduced to an arid ruin, a visual reminder that Ahab and Jezebel had turned the land into a spiritual ruin.

God's people do suffer in this sinful world. But often they experience miracles on their behalf, as in the case of Elijah. A shaggy black bird of the wilderness—a bird that was "unclean" according to the Israelite kosher laws—became the means of sustaining the physical life of one of the Lord's great prophets.

Organic (and Recycled) Food in Famine Time

Were they "seed pods" or really what the Bible says they were?

Famine is still a feature of human life, even though it shouldn't be, for the world produces enough food to feed everyone. Technology has advanced, and so has agricultural science, yet still people starve. And if things are bad today, it was worse in the ancient world, where people were even more at the mercy of floods or droughts.

But of course, some humans cause some famines—specifically, with sieges that cut off cities from outside food supplies. In 2 Kings we learn that Ben-Hadad, the king of Aram, besieged Samaria, the capital city of Israel at that time. Here is 2 Kings 6:25, in the King James Version: "And there was a great famine in Samaria; and behold, they besieged it, until an ass's head was sold for fourscore pieces of silver, and the fourth part of a cab of dove's dung for five pieces of silver."

"Dove's dung"—meaning *bird droppings?* Possibly. The original Hebrew words literally mean "dove's dung." But modern translators think that may have been a slang expression meaning "seed pods" or "wild onions"—in either case, a plant that only the very poorest folk normally ate. We aren't sure, though those suggestions sound more likely than bird droppings. As for the donkey's head, yes, it was highly probable that starving people would eat such things. The donkey was, by the way, nonkosher for the Israelites—but under siege they didn't care.

But stranger food than donkey's heads was being consumed. A woman of the city spoke to the king himself and told him how desperate things had become: "This woman said to me, 'Give up your son so we may eat him today, and tomorrow we'll eat my son.' So we cooked my son and ate him. The next day I said to her, 'Give up your son so we may eat him,' but she had hidden him" (2 Kings 6:28–29).

225

Mercy. Hunger had reduced the people to cannibalism. Sounds horrible, but we have no reason to think that 2 Kings 6 is fiction, for history records that people have done such things. Eating one's own children sounds like something out of a Grimm's fairy tale—or a horror movie. But 2 Kings sets the whole matter in context: the famine had occurred because of the nation's immorality. It is a familiar theme in the Old Testament: if you do bad things, bad things will happen to you.

The Ancient Version of Workplace Theft

Achan, who sinned badly and was then achin'

Y ou have heard the word *harem*, no doubt, and you know it applies to the part of a Middle Eastern home where the wives and concubines stayed to themselves (except when entertaining their master, that is). It comes from an Arabic word meaning "prohibited" or "off-limits"—for this area was off-limits to all men except the master of the house. The word relates to a word in the Hebrew Bible, a word that plays a prominent—and sometimes fatal—role in the book of Joshua.

The Hebrew word was *herem*, and it is almost impossible to translate, but it meant something like "set aside," "devoted to," or "consecrated to." When the Israelites under Joshua came into Canaan, the land God had promised them, they were told that when they captured a Canaanite city, everything in it was *herem* "to the Lord"—meaning that everything was to be dedicated to God, not for the people's private use. In other words, the Israelites were not to use the move into Canaan as an opportunity to steal and pillage. In fact, the rule of thumb when taking a Canaanite city was: destroy everything.

This impresses some people as rather silly. If you capture a city, why destroy all its supplies and other valuables? Why not put them to good use? Sounds sensible from a human point of view, but God saw it differently: his chosen people, the Israelites, must not turn into a band of thieving marauders. By destroying the Canaanites' things instead of keeping them for their own use, they would be reminded of why they were there in the first place: to settle the land and worship the one true God. Also, had they spared the Canaanites' goods, among them they would have found plenty of idols—and these would have been a temptation to follow false gods.

Before the dramatic capture of the city of Jericho, God issued Joshua a stern warning about the *herem* rule:

> The city and all that is in it are to be devoted to the LORD . . . But keep away from the devoted [*herem*] things, so that you will not bring about your own destruction by taking any of them. Otherwise you will make the camp of Israel liable to destruction and bring trouble on it. (Josh. 6:17–18)

They could keep some gold and silver articles to use in the worship of God, but they must destroy everything else.

Well, human nature is what it is, and inevitably some Israelite would decide that God wouldn't mind (or wouldn't know) if he kept some of the goods of Jericho for himself. The one who did was a man named Achan. "So the LORD's anger burned against Israel" (Josh. 7:1).

Pause a moment here and consider the whole notion of sin. We think of it as an individual matter, and it is as individuals that we will all finally be judged. But at the time of Joshua, God was deeply concerned about the whole community of Israel. He was trying to shape his chosen people into a force for good in the world, so they had to be good collectively as well as individually. If one of them sinned, it was a blot on the whole nation—the "one rotten apple spoils the bunch" phenomenon.

So, though it seems odd to us, God was angry at all the Israelites for what Achan had done. And so he punished the whole group of them, and in a dramatic way. After the triumph at Jericho, the people expected further triumphs. But the next attempt to take a city, the city of Ai, was a total failure. Several Israelite men died, and the people lost heart. They thought they were on a winning streak, but they were wrong.

Joshua mourned and wailed and asked God what was wrong. God was blunt: Israel had sinned by not destroying everything in Jericho. The Israelites would not capture any more cities till they had removed the sin—which meant removing Achan, though Joshua did not yet know it.

The next morning Joshua was to examine each tribe of Israel to find the man (or men) who had violated the *herem* rule. It came out that Achan was the man. Achan admitted what he had done. While in the city he had spotted a beautiful robe, a stash of gold, and a stash of silver. He "coveted them and took them" (Josh. 7:21) and buried them in the ground inside his tent. Joshua sent some men to the tent, and sure enough, there was Achan's loot.

He was guilty as charged, and Israel stoned him—along with his entire family and even his livestock—to death. As a kind of vivid reminder of Achan's fate, they heaped a big pile of rocks on his grave.

"Then the LORD turned from his fierce anger" (Josh. 7:26). As proof of that, the next chapter relates that the Israelites captured the city of Ai. Having gotten rid of the sinner Achan, things could now go well for Israel.

Do you think this story makes God look bad? Many readers do. A man stoned to death just because he snatched a robe and some money from a burning city? Sounds like a major punishment for a minor crime. But the author of Joshua didn't see it that way. Had Achan gotten away with his theft, he would probably have done it again—and others would have learned about it, and probably done the same, so long as they thought that God did not see what they had done. If such theft had continued, the Israelites would have turned into just another band of desert thieves, attacking cities so as to make off with the goods. And that wasn't why God had brought them to Canaan.

We talk a lot today about the "deterrent effect" of punishing criminals. We can safely assume that Achan's very public death had an effect on all the other Israelites. There is no further mention in Joshua of any Israelite violating the *herem* rule.

Any moral lessons in this bizarre, gory story? Sure. One is, always be mindful that God is watching. Each of us is tempted to "do an Achan" now and then, committing a "petty sin" that we figure will go unnoticed. But maybe our petty sins are not so petty after all. We aren't going to be stoned to death as Achan was, but any sin great or small has an effect on our character, and on our walk with God.

Earthly Powers Versus the Rebels

— ◆ —

A man named Korah, who was truly down-to-earth

Bible readers all know and respect the amazing Moses, God's man appointed to lead the Israelite slaves out of Egypt. But the poor man faced continual griping and occasional rebellion. One of these rebellions was the one Korah led, and Numbers 16 describes it. Korah had 250 fellow rebels, all men of high standing, and the group rebelled against the leadership of Moses and his brother Aaron.

Like many rebellions, this one was based on envy: the rebels hated the men at the top and wanted them toppled.

This was an intertribal matter, for the rebels, like Moses and Aaron, were from the tribe of Levi. The Levites were Israel's "priestly" tribe, and when the Israelites eventually settled in Canaan, it was the Levites who served not only as priests but as aides and musicians in God's temple. Korah and his fellow rebels thought all the Levites ought to be equal in rank with Moses. And Moses—and God—did not agree.

A sort of showdown was staged—an incense showdown. Moses, Aaron, and the rebels were to appear in front of the Tent of Meeting, the large tent that was the center of Israel's worship at that time. Each man was to have with him a censer—an incense burner, that is. The Lord himself appeared (not visibly, but somehow they all knew he was there) and told Moses he was going to put an end to the rebellion—by putting an end to the rebels.

Moses, always the compassionate soul, begged for mercy on the rebels. But God instructed Moses to tell the other Israelites to move away from their rebels' tents, for something horrible was about to happen. So Moses made a brief speech to the assembly, telling them that if the rebels died a natural death, "then the LORD has not sent me" (Num. 16:29).

> As soon as he finished saying all this, the ground under them split apart, and the earth opened its mouth and swallowed them, with their households and all Korah's men and all their possessions. They went down alive into the grave, with everything they owned; the earth closed over them, and they perished and were gone from the community. (Num. 16:31–33)

Then, a dramatic finish: "And fire came out from the LORD and consumed the 250 men who were offering the incense" (Num. 16:35).

At the time of the earthquake and fire, the Israelites were trembling with fear. The next morning, however, they were in a totally different mood: they were complaining against Moses and Aaron, saying they had "killed the LORD's people" (Num. 16:41). A truly bizarre complaint, when it was clear that Moses and Aaron had not caused the earthquake and fire. To punish the gripers, the Lord struck the people with a plague, and 14,700 died.

A strange story, and one that makes us think ill of the Lord. But try to look at it from the perspective of the Bible authors—and the perspective of God. If God had allowed any of the rebellions against Moses to proceed, he would never have taken the Israelites all the way to Canaan. They would have ended up there in the wilderness, probably turning into a band of nomadic raiders, like the many tribes that harassed them in those days.

Moses and Aaron were God's men, and the people had seen enough miracles performed that they should have been convinced of that. Their ingratitude toward God and Moses was unbearable, and God had to send a clear signal: *Stick with Moses, people, he is the right man for the job.* We can hardly believe that the grousing Korah or anyone else among the rebels would have been up to the task of leading these ex-slaves through the wilderness for forty years.